ALL CHANGE
at
OLD TRAFFORD

ALL CHANGE
at
OLD TRAFFORD

THE FRANK O'FARRELL STORY

by FRANK O'FARRELL

with Jeff Welch

THANKS

This book could not have been written without the help of a long list of people, not least all my former team-mates and the players whom I managed during my career. I thank them for playing a part in my story. Special thanks also to Nigel Biddlecombe (Weymouth FC), Ian Rigby (Preston Former Players Association), Finbarr Buckley, Bob Bond, Ivan Ponting, Frank Grande, Julian Pugh, Phil Chard, Tommy Docherty, Dave Thomas, Tony McDonald, Tony Drummond, Tommy Spratt, Tommy Thompson, John Bond, John Farrington, Martin Buchan, Ted MacDougall, Peter Coady, Mike Berry & Sandra Nicholson at BACKPASS football magazine (www.backpassmagazine.co.uk) and www.soccerscene.ie

Frank's co-author Jeff Welch is a former BBC Radio and Westcountry TV reporter, based in Devon, but originally from Cumbria. He supports Barrow AFC.

The front cover picture of a steam engine is *Maeve*, an 800 class 4-6-0 locomotive used on the Cork to Dublin line in the 1940s.

First published in Great Britain in 2011

Printed and managed by Jellyfish Print Solutions

All enquiries to hello@backpassmagazine.co.uk

ISBN 978-0-9570118-0-9

CONTENTS

This book is dedicated to my wife Ann,
who has been my rock and guiding light.

Frank and Ann O'Farrell have been married for 57 years.

FOREWORD

IN ALL my many years in football, I don't think I ever met anyone quite like Frank O'Farrell.

I played both against him and with him for Preston North End, and later I succeeded him as manager of Manchester United.

As a player, he was a very talented wing-half, a terrific man marker and an excellent user of the ball. Whatever role he was asked to undertake, Frank did it to the letter. He was a true professional in every sense.

As a manager Frank's career stalled during his 18 months at Old Trafford and I believe Manchester United treated him very shabbily. He wasn't given the backing to make the changes that were badly needed at the time, and I don't think some of the senior players at the club helped the situation.

The circumstances of me taking over from Frank as manager of Manchester United have been well chronicled over the years.

I had gone to the game at Crystal Palace in December 1972, which proved to be Frank's final match in charge, as manager of the Scottish national team and I was very surprised to be approached at half-time by Louis Edwards and Matt Busby and asked if I wanted to be manager of Manchester United.

When I told them they already had a manager, they said they wouldn't have by Wednesday. I rang Frank when I got home that night and put him in the picture, and asked him what I should do. He said I had to take the job.

I think for both Frank and me, it was a case of being in the right place at the wrong time - or the wrong place at the right time!

To Frank's credit, we never fell out over it and we have remained lifelong friends. Frank and his wife Ann are lovely people, and Frank was even a godfather to one of my children.

I still see Frank every year at the annual Preston North End Former Players Association dinner and it is always a pleasure to meet up with him again.

He is one of the very best ... and I love him to bits.

TOMMY DOCHERTY

INTRODUCTION

MY CAREER in football almost happened by accident. As a teenager in Ireland, I never had any aspirations of playing professionally, let alone managing Manchester United.

Instead I wanted to be a steam engine driver like my father. It was my one goal in life.

I never went in search of fame and fortune as that was never my nature. Hopefully this book will show that.

I was just fortunate how things developed in my football career. One minute I was happily playing for Cork United, the next I was at West Ham United. I was then happy to be player-manager of non-League Weymouth - but within six years I was manager of the mighty Manchester United.

Amazingly, although it is 40 years ago, I still meet strangers who ask me about my time at Old Trafford, as if it was a defining moment in my life, and I wanted to write this book to put the record straight.

My spell in charge of Manchester United was certainly a time when I enjoyed the highest possible profile, but whether it was an enjoyable time or not is another matter.

All Change at Old Trafford is not just about the 18 months I spent at one of the biggest clubs in the world alongside the likes of Matt Busby, George Best, Bobby Charlton and Denis Law.

It's about a small boy from a humble background in Ireland who grew up desperately wanting to follow in his father's footsteps on the railway - yet who somehow got shunted on to a totally different career path.

I hope you enjoy the ride ... I certainly have.

FRANK O'FARRELL

EVENTS OF 1927

Charles Lindbergh made the first solo transatlantic flight
from New York to Paris.

Pope Benedict XVI was born.

In Britain, 1,000 people a week died from an influenza epidemic.

The Jazz Singer opened to herald the decline of the silent movie era.

The BBC broadcast their first live sports commentary from the
England v Wales rugby union match at Twickenham.

Francis O'Farrell was born in Cork, Ireland on October 9th.

1

WHEN IRISH EYES ARE SMILING

Hail to thee, blithe Spirit,
Bird thou never wert,
That from Heaven or near it,
Pourest thy full heart,
In profuse strains of unpremeditated art ...

Percy Bysshe Shelley

THEY say life is one big journey and mine started on October 9th, 1927, when I was born in an area in the north of the city of Cork in Ireland called Blackpool.

I was christened Francis, though this was later shortened to Frank, and I was the fifth child of eight. I think my mother, Catherine, was quite pleased to see me as I was a boy after a run of three girls. I had an elder brother, Patrick, but then my mum had had three daughters, Maureen, Josie and Kitty. Then after me came Matthew, James and my youngest sister Anne. Five of us are still alive; Patrick, the eldest of the eight who worked in the civil service, Kitty and my eldest sister Maureen have sadly passed on.

Rather than say times were hard, I would describe my early years as frugal. My father, Patrick, who was in hospital with scarlet fever when I was born, was a fireman on the railway at the time, and he later became an engine driver. It was heavy, back-breaking work at a time when there was not much employment around, but it was a secure job.

Both my mum and dad were from Cork, from the area where we were born. We were from the north side of the city, and there was always a great sporting rivalry between the north side and the south, which was divided by the River Lee.

We lived in pretty poor accommodation above a sweet shop and one of my earliest recollections was when I was about four. The railway was at the bottom of our small garden and I wanted to give my dad a sweet when his train went by. Of course he couldn't take it and I got quite upset. He'd wave to me and I'd wave back, but on this day I just wanted to give him a sweet.

I used to see my grandparents a lot, and my grandfather on my father's side, also Patrick, was a good musician, and a very well-educated man. He played the clarinet and violin and I remember attending his funeral when I was about 11 and walking behind the hearse with all the other men, as was the custom of the time. My grandmother was Mary, and they were often called the Farrells rather than the O'Farrells. I used to be called Frankie Farrell at times without using the O.

My grandmother on my mother's side was also Mary, which was a popular name in honour of Mary, the Mother of our Lord, and my maternal grandfather was Matt. He worked in Murphy's Brewery, which is now owned by Heineken, and he had been a merchant seaman. He used to tell me stories about his travels to places like Hong Kong and Shanghai.

He told me one tale about an old Chinese chap who came up to him at the dockside one time with a small monkey on his back. He wanted to swap the monkey for my granddad's black coat. The Chinaman said "Changey for changey Sam? A good old new coat for a black monkey?"

There were six of us kids living above the sweet shop, and times were tough. When I was born I am told the Sisters of the Poor, a religious order of nuns in Blackpool who assisted poor families, helped my mother as my father was in hospital.

In 1932, when I was five, the Cork Corporation built a new estate and we were rehoused from the north to the south of the city to a place called Turner's Cross.

I had started school a few months earlier at Blackpool Boys' School, and at the time there was no school near the new estate, so I went to the South Monastery in Douglas Street, which was run by the Presentation Brothers and about a mile's walk, before I switched to the newly-built Christ the King School, which was opened in 1938. It was just a short walk at the bottom of Friars Road, where we lived.

The houses had three bedrooms, but no bathroom. We used to go down to the local baths once a week to have a shower or bath. Three of us boys slept in one room - three to a double bed - and the three girls also had their own bedroom. It used to get very cold at night, there was no central heating, and we would put overcoats over the blankets on the bed to keep warm. There was often frost on the inside of the windows in the mornings during winter.

At school, I was always in the top five or six in the class, and we would do tests at Easter and Christmas and I would always win a book, or a hurley, a long stick for playing hurling. Many of the subjects were taught in Irish, because it was a time when the Irish Government was trying to foster and redevelop the language again after it has been banned by the English!

Coming up to do the Intermediate Examination, when we were about 10 or 11, we started Latin through the medium of Irish.

We had to plough through Caesar's Gallic Wars and Virgil's Aenaid in preparation for our exams.

In 1941 myself and another classmate, Sean O'Brien, were selected to sit an oral and written test in Irish language at the School of Art. Whichever of us got the best marks in the test would then represent our school, Christ the King, in spending a month at a summer school in Ballingeary, a village in the Shehy Mountains in West Cork, studying

Frank's parents, Patrick and Catherine.

Irish along with pupils from other schools. Ballingeary at that time was one of a number of places in Ireland where the Irish language had survived and was spoken all the time.

I was surprised to beat Sean in the test as he was a very clever boy, and a lovely person who later studied for the priesthood in the order of Mill Hill Fathers, and went out on the mission to New Zealand.

Also at Ballingeary was a boy who lived in the same road as me. His name was Liam O'Murchú and he was representing the North Monastery, a Christian Brothers' school in Cork. He was a brilliant scholar and came first in the All-Ireland exams and subsequently joined the Civil Service and had an Irish language chat programme on Radio Eireann called Trom agus Eadrom (which means heavy and light).

At the sports day at Ballingeary, Liam and me won the three-legged race, and some years later when we met again he gave me a mild rebuke because I had insisted on sharing the prize, which was a box of chocolates, with the other competitors! I had forgotten all about that.

I also won another prize, though I can't remember what it was, for a poc fada or long puck. I hit the ball, or sliothar, with the hurley the furthest. The whole experience at Ballingeary was wonderful. We were all billeted in different farmhouses, and Liam and me were with a very welcoming family named Healy.

At the South Monastery, my first school in South Cork, one of the lay teachers who taught us was called Gerald Fitzgerald, who also played for the Lees Club, and he was influential in introducing me to Gaelic football. We only had a small playground, and the facilities were quite basic, but he taught us positional play, ball sense, jumping, accuracy and above all, competitiveness. You didn't squeal at the bodily contact - and there was plenty of it.

A lot of top Irish footballers, like Johnny Carey and Noel Cantwell, began as Gaelic footballers and I am proud to have done the same.

The brothers at the new Christ the King school, like the South Monastery a boys' school, lived in the community at the monastery. It was their calling to do what they were doing and I always thought they were quite inspiring and very dedicated.

They used to walk a mile to the school every day, whatever the weather, and often their shoes were falling apart. They didn't make any money out of it - it was their vocation. They devoted their lives to educating poor children and if we occasionally got the cane, we never held it against them.

To be honest, we were never aware we were poor, and we were better off than a lot of other families. Some of the other dads had no jobs and some had come back from the First World War and were still struggling to find work. But compared to today's kids, our dreams and expectations were so totally different.

During the summer, my father was entitled to six free passes on the railway and we used them to go to the lovely seaside town of Youghal. We would walk a couple of miles down to the station carrying our bags of food for the day to catch the train, and sit on the beach all day long.

My mother would often bring a child with us from another of the poor families in our neighbourhood. Years later some of them told me that had it not been for my mother, they would never have seen Youghal when they were young. My mum was like that, very considerate and charitable. She would also have me deliver food parcels, sharing what we had with families who were worse off than us.

The only person who had a car in our street was the owner of the local grocer's shop, but we were never unhappy as children.

During the Second World War, gas was rationed though you could still use it as they couldn't cut it off totally. You weren't supposed to use it, but we did. We also had a coal fire, but coal became scarce as well, and we had to burn turf. The turf was usually quite dry and hard, but sometimes it was damp and I can remember my mother, God rest her soul, on her knees blowing to try and spark the fire to life.

Turner's Cross was near the country in an area known as the Black Ash, and in the summer it was paradise. There was a stream that we dammed up to make our own swimming pool, and we would stay there all day long. We used to eat the berries from the hawthorn trees and pinch the odd turnip from the farmer's field. It may have been a frugal time but my memories are such happy ones.

At school we learned Shelley's poetry, and I particularly

remember Ode to a Skylark.

It went *Hail to thee, blithe Spirit, Bird thou never wert, That from Heaven or near it, Pourest thy full heart, In profuse strains of unpremeditated art. Higher still and higher, From the earth thou springest, Like a cloud of fire, The blue deep thou wingest, And singing still dost soar, and soaring ever singest.*

We often used to lie in the grass under the hot sun drying off from swimming looking and listening to the skylarks. Shelley wrote that beautiful poem in Italy, and he too must have been sitting in the sun like us at the time looking into the sky listening to skylarks.

In the autumn we would go blackberrying, and we would sell the blackberries to the local jam factory, Ogilvie and Moore. We used to cheat a little by putting water in the can or bucket, so they were heavier and we got paid more. Mea culpa!

We also used to pick mushrooms. I had a friend called Finbarr Long, whose father was a postman, and who used to get him up before he went on his round, and Finbarr in turn would knock me up and we would go picking mushrooms before school. Sadly Finbarr died of tuberculosis when he was about 15. I used to visit him in hospital before he died and it was a very sad time for me - he was one of my best friends.

We were always out playing, swimming, climbing trees or collecting conkers. In winter if there was a hard frost we'd put water down on the road and we'd have an ice-skating rink. There were few cars on the roads in those days. It was all great fun, though the problem was the milkman, Tom Mulcahy, coming the following morning with his horse, and not being able to get up the road. He'd have to put bags on the horse's feet to stop them from slipping and not surprisingly he wasn't happy about it.

We were always active. There was no television and we didn't have a lot of games or toys so once our homework was done, we were free. We'd find things to do - and it kept us fit.

Once I was swimming at the local open-air baths, a place called Victoria Cross that has long since closed and has had a hotel built on the site. The base of the baths wasn't tiled, it was concreted so you couldn't see the bottom, and there was a shallow end and a deep end. I was in the shallow end but somehow wandered into the deep end without realising I was drowning and someone had to pull me out. His name was Sean Quinn and he lived near me in Evergreen Road. He saw my predicament and dived in to pull me out and they had to pump the water from me. Sean was older than me, I'd probably be about 10 I suppose, and I knew at the time I needed help. There were people around as it was a lovely day, and someone spotted what was happening. Sean pulled me out and one of the attendants sat me down and squished the water out of me - it was a near miss.

I don't think I told my parents - my mum might not have let me go up there again! That would be the first of three near-death experiences I would have in my life.

I was born into a Catholic family, went to Catholic schools, learned my faith and saw the examples my parents set. Practising the Catholic faith has always been natural for me, but I don't go out of my way to push it down other people's throats or anything like that. I sang as an alto in the church choir and I've always been comfortable with my faith, although I prefer the traditional old Latin Mass more than the new, even though I have been denied access to it for much of the last 40 years, in spite of Pope Benedict stating in 2007 that that form of the Mass had never been abrogated, and in principle was always available.

Religion has played a big part in my life. I started going to Mass when I was five or six and I am now 84 and still go most days. These are my values and I try to uphold them.

As a boy, I was into several sports, and my father was a big follower as well. When Jimmy Braddock famously beat Max Baer in New York in 1935 to win the World Boxing title, my father knocked us up to tell us about it when he got in from work early that morning.

He would tell me about all the great English and Scottish footballers, and he was a big Glasgow Celtic fan. He was interested in hurling as well, supporting the St Finbarrs club, and used to take me to matches. I played football, Gaelic football and hurling as a schoolboy, and we also played throwing bowls, a sport in which my grand-uncle on my mother's side, Jack McGrath, or 'Buck' as they called him, was a legend.

There was a lot of betting on the sport, which saw two men throwing a 28 ounce iron bowl down unmade roads for a mile or so. Buck is reputed to be the only man to have cleared a very high

Grand-uncle 'Buck' McGrath was a legendary bowler.

railway viaduct outside Cork with one of these bowls. Later he emigrated to America and never came back, but they still talk about him even now in Cork, he's a legend in the sport. As young boys, we used to play bowls with a 16 ounce bowl.

Most Saturdays I would go to watch football at Turner's Cross, and I recall being there and listening to the 1938 FA Cup final between Preston and Huddersfield Town on a radio at a nearby house. It was the final where Preston's George Mutch scored the winner from the penalty spot in the last minute of extra-time. Little did I realise at the time that I would one day play for the great Preston North End.

I was captain of my Gaelic football team at Christ the King, and we did well in winning a trophy only two years after the school opened. We took some beatings early on, but we improved and when we beat the North Monastery, a well-established school, in the final it was a great triumph.

It was the first sporting trophy Christ the King had won, and the school went on to subsequently produce many top-class sportsmen, like Marcus O'Sullivan, the great Olympic miler, and Billy Morgan, who played for the Cork Gaelic football team and then successfully coached and managed the team after retiring.

I also started playing schoolboy soccer for Nicholas Rovers on Sundays. If you played Gaelic football, you weren't supposed to play soccer as well so it had to be done on the quiet. You faced a ban, or even six of the best for playing this 'foreign' game, but the brothers at the school mostly turned a blind eye and didn't make an issue of it.

A man named Mr Madden ran Nicholas Rovers, his son Seamus played and so did Peter Desmond, who went on to play for Middlesbrough and was in the Irish team who famously beat England 2-0 at Goodison Park in 1949. I played left-half and we were a decent side. My mum and dad would come and watch occasionally, but they never put any pressure on me, it was mainly just "how did you get on?"

One of my early sporting heroes was Jack Lynch, who later became the Prime Minister of Ireland. He was a great hurler with Glen Rovers, and years later when I was made Texaco Sports Personality of the Year in Dublin for 1971, he presented me with the prize. That was a real honour for me.

Christie Ring and Shaun Condon were also fantastic hurlers. Christie used to drive a lorry for Esso and he'd take his hurling stick along with him. When he had a break on the road, he'd go off into an empty field and start practising his shots - he was a really fine player.

As far as football went, among my favourites players were

Frank, in the centre of the seated row behind the ball, was captain of the Gaelic football team at Christ the King school in 1940.

19

Sean McCarthy, a centre-forward, Liam O'Neill and Owen Madden.

My elder brother joined the post office after leaving school, becoming a telegram boy and then a telegraph clerk, and my sister Maureen worked in a chemist's shop, mainly developing films. My other sister Josie worked at the Sunbeam Wolsey textile factory in Cork and my younger brother Jimmy went to England and worked at Ford in Dagenham. He was a decent footballer and had a trial with Arsenal. He also won an All-Ireland schoolboy medal with the Evergreen club.

I left school at 15 and wanted to follow my dad and become an engine driver, but I couldn't start on the railway until I was 16. I was now playing for Clapton Celtic in the minor league. I messed about for a year until I could join the railway, and Pat Downing, a plumber who ran Clapton Celtic, gave me a few bob to help him out plumbing. I didn't do much though - it was more of a bribe to play I think.

We played at a place called Douglas and next to the pitch was a stream where we could wash all the mud off afterwards. There were changing rooms but no running water so we certainly weren't molly-coddled. There were no bathing facilities, just a place to change and leave your clothes to keep dry while you were playing. It was fun, but it was tough.

Then another team, Western Rovers, asked me if I'd sign for them. Neil Welsh ran Western Rovers - he was a Protestant and we also had two Jewish lads playing for us as well. One of them, Ivor Scher, was from a family of dentists and he also became a dentist. Years later when I was at Leicester I met him again at a game in Bournemouth, where he had set up a practice. He later went to work on a kibbutz in Israel.

The rest of us, including Noel Cantwell's elder brother, Frank, were all Catholics, and one of the team, Jim McGrath, went on to become a priest, joining the Columban fathers and going out to South Korea as a missioner. He was a terrific person but sadly died out there at a relatively young age. When the World Cup was held in South Korea in 2002, there was a newspaper article about how he had helped develop football in the country.

Jim had a brother, Pat, who also played for Western Rovers, who were in the same league as Clapton Celtic. If you were successful and got to cup finals, they were played at a local senior club's ground, where they had the luxury of changing rooms with baths. We won a couple of cups and it was a very enjoyable time.

I finally joined the railway as an engine cleaner when I was 16 and continued to play junior football for Western Rovers. I also played for the railway team in an inter-house league that included quite a few semi-professionals. I must have done well because that was when Cork United asked me if I'd join them in August 1947.

One of their senior players was Owen Madden. He had played for Norwich City and Birmingham City before the War, and then come back to Ireland. I think it was Owen who approached me to see if I'd sign for Cork. I went to see the directors and they offered me £3 per week, plus £1 for a win and 10 shillings for a draw. I felt I was a rich man - this was on top of my railway money, which was another £3 a week.

We played at the Mardyke, then the premier ground in Cork but one that is no longer used. It belonged to University College. This was a real step-up. I was playing with other professionals like Owen and Sean McCarthy, and some of them were full-timers

A 16-year-old Frank (third from the left on the back row) pictured in a Western Rovers team shot in 1943. Frank Cantwell, Noel's older brother, is second from the right at the front.

who trained every day. I learned so much from Owen. He taught me about positioning and seeing ahead in the game, reading the game he called it. He'd say "Before you get the ball, know what you're going to do with it. You've got to have a picture in your mind."

I was playing in front of bigger crowds of around 3,000 and I got my name in the papers more. Reading through the reports was always important for your self-esteem. We played the other semi-professional clubs like Shamrock Rovers, Shelbourne, Waterford and Limerick.

I had a pretty good run. I started in August 1947 and played for six months. We did quite well, and it was a great time for me. Doing two jobs, I enjoyed getting paid very well, living at home - and going dancing!

I replaced Tommy Moroney at Cork as he'd gone to West Ham in the August along with Johnny McGowan. Tommy was a fine player, not only at football but at rugby as well. I watched him play but never played with him until I got to West Ham.

Johnny, who was a right-back, had a wonderful personality and was always smiling. I saw him a few years ago when I went over to Ireland for my brother-in-law's funeral. He came over to the Requiem Mass as he knew I'd be home. Sadly he too has since passed away.

The teenage Frank O'Farrell growing up in Cork. Frank is pictured on the left at 16 years of age and then right, aged 18 in 1945.
Frank left school at the age of 15 and started on the railway as a cleaner, with a view to becoming a fireman and then a driver.

I had watched Cork play regularly so it was a bit of a dream come true to play for them. We used to go up there as boys to watch the matches and ask someone to take us through the turnstile. If we couldn't get someone to take us in, we'd walk up to a local wood called Shanakiel Wood and watch from up there. It was like looking down from a bird's eye view.

I was getting a bit more known around Cork and it was my first taste of fame. But the 'star' thing wasn't like it is today. We accepted what we did in a more balanced sort of way and never went over the top. We just accepted and enjoyed it while it lasted.

I had my heart set on becoming an engine driver like my dad, but first you had to learn the ropes as a fireman. I saw it as a secure job that would have lasted until I was pensioned off at the age of 65.

That was my ambition and it was a reasonable ambition at the time. The fact that my father was a driver helped me to get into the profession. It was a sort of tradition that sons of engine drivers followed their fathers and became engine drivers too.

But eventually steam engines were phased out and replaced by diesel and electric engines so had I stayed on the railway and qualified as a driver, there would have been no steam engines to drive.

I was a cleaner for two years and then I became a fireman - that's the route you took to becoming a driver. First you clean the engines to make them all spick and span, and then you become a fireman.

I was stationed in Mallow for a while and I'd go back to Cork to play football on a Saturday. There were no trains on Sundays so I used to borrow my brother's bike and cycle back to Mallow (about 30 miles) along a dark, unlit road. It was so dark at times that I ended up in the ditch more than once.

We did all sorts of different runs, one of which was down to Waterford where we used to take the sugar beet trains, and also down to the sugar beet factory in Mallow.

During the War you couldn't get cane sugar in from Jamaica, so there was a big movement to grow your own food. Ireland was neutral at the time and it was difficult to get foodstuffs so they opened up the beet factories and we'd take the wagons of sugar beet down to be processed into sugar. It was very hard work.

First of all you would go down to the locomotive shed and get allocated your engine. It would be pretty well full of steam because they had people allocated to do that who were called 'steam risers'. Then we'd have to oil the engines - they were very big - and the axles. Then you had to build the fire up in order to get enough steam for when you latched onto a train, whether it was passenger or goods.

Steam trains were a bit like football teams and could be very temperamental. You could take an engine out and it would be a real joy - the fire would burn beautifully and you'd have excess steam rising up through the exhaust valve. Then you could take the same engine out the next day and it wouldn't do that and you'd be grafting and wouldn't have enough steam. Some drivers were better at nursing the engine along than others.

The hardest day's work I ever did was on a sugar beet train up from Tralee to Mallow. The coal we had was low-grade as England was at war and they kept the best stuff for industry. It didn't burn efficiently, didn't make steam and you had to clean the fires out on the journey.

There was an innovation called a drop bar that allowed you to get rid of the clinker at the bottom of the fire box, rather than dig it out with steel shovels, by lifting it and dropping it on to the track underneath.

Now there was a particular type of engine, a 359, that didn't have these drop bars and on this one trip from Tralee to Mallow I had to clean the fire out three times and I was absolutely shattered. You had to open the firebox and clean it out with a big long steel shovel. You put the burning coals on the left on top of the hot fire on the right. Under that was a layer of clinker and you had to break it up sufficiently small to bring it through the firebox door. Then you'd dump it down the side, move the live coals over to the other side and do the same again with the clinker on that side. Then you had to spread the live coals around and build up the fire by adding more coal as it burned. The memory of that night has never left me - I was totally exhausted when I got home.

I worked on a train with my father just the once. My father was a very efficient driver and a very conscientious man - my mother used to say he was married to his job. He'd get down to the locomotive shed long before he had to clock on and was never

Frank (top right) pictured on the railway with his father in front of him, and below with his father Patrick next to him standing highest on the engine. The fireman is Conny Lynch. The bottom picture was taken at Amiens Street Station in Dublin when Frank was back home for an international match.

late for his work. I like to feel I took after him in that way. He was a fine gentleman.

The hours depended on what time the train was going out. If it was a goods train it could be 9 or 10 o'clock at night, or it could be 6 or 8 o'clock in the morning. My mother had a built-in alarm clock - any time of the night you had to be up she'd call you, even it was 2 or 3 in the morning.

There was also a man known as the caller-upper. He'd go round on his bicycle and knock on your door or throw a stone at your window. There were no alarm clocks or mobile phones in those days.

The hours were mostly irregular, but the superintendent, Simon Murphy, usually let me off at weekends because I was playing football. He was very helpful that way. He wasn't a football fan but when I signed semi-professional with Cork United he used to arrange a different shift or swap with someone else so I could travel up to Dublin or wherever for the away matches.

If I was working in the afternoon, I'd train in the morning. If I worked in the morning, then I would train in the evening.

One valuable lesson I learned when I was a cleaner was never put a case to anyone unless you could back it up with a strong argument. Gerry Cunningham was the engine cleaners' foreman and he allocated the different jobs at the beginning of the shift.

On one occasion he told me I had to clean the back of an engine which had come in from Limerick. Usually when an engine came from Limerick, it was pretty filthy. Now I was being sent to clean one of those engines and it would mean me squatting down in the pit under the engine and making my way from the front to where the firebox was, and I just didn't fancy it.

So I told Gerry I couldn't get in there to start cleaning because of the way the engine was parked. It was not a good argument and I knew it really - I just didn't want to do it. Gerry said "I'll show you how to get in" and he did so with little trouble - and he had a wooden leg! The moral of the story is never try it on unless you can back it up.

I was on the railway for four years and things were going very well. I had two wages coming in and I felt I was in clover. I was living at home, had plenty of friends in what was a lovely city. Then in 1947 West Ham came and messed it all up!

Tommy Moroney and Johnny McGowan had both left Cork to join the Hammers in August 1947, with money changing hands, and someone told me they were now interested in me.

A scout named Ben Ives, who had been responsible for Tommy and Johnny joining West Ham, came to see me. He'd already been to see me play. I was playing well for Cork, and enjoying myself, and to be honest I wasn't gushing with enthusiasm to leave. I said I was going to be an engine driver and I was enjoying my football.

He said he thought I could make the grade and he seemed a very sincere man. He told me that Tommy and Johnny had settled well in London and did I want to join them? I asked what the fee was and he said they would be paying Cork United £3,000 - which was quite a lot of money then.

He told me my basic wage would be £10 per week, and I'd get an extra £2 if I played in the first team. The maximum wage at the time was £12 a week. I asked the Cork United directors that if

Cork United in 1947, with Frank, now 20, third from the left on the back row. Owen Madden is sat in the centre at the front and Sean McCarthy is on the far right on the front row. Tony Drummond, who talks about Frank at the back of the book (page 168), is at the far left on the back row.

they were going to get £3,000 from the deal, what would I be getting? I said I wanted £1,000 and I got it. That was like a fortune to me. I would never have saved that sort of money if I'd been shovelling coal for the engines.

I felt I was making a big sacrifice to give up my dream of becoming an engine driver. If I was to leave the railway I might not be able to get back into it again - and I could be a failure at West Ham. Therefore I needed some financial insurance. I think the Cork chairman was a bit taken aback but he was still getting £2,000. I felt like a millionaire when I went to the bank and put my £1,000 in.

The railway bosses were very understanding and wished me well. I got my back pay and a very nice reference from them - and I still have that reference to this day.

I was nervous about going to London. I was 20 and it was a big decision to leave my home, my friends and my family behind. It was like going into the unknown and a foreign environment. I'd lived in Cork with some protection from my family and friends, but the fact that Tommy and Johnny had gone before me helped. I had always looked up to both of them.

Everything was sorted out in the December but I actually went over in January 1948. Tommy and Johnny had a spare week because West Ham had been knocked out of the FA Cup and had been home to Ireland for a short break, so I travelled back with them on the ferry from Cork to Fishguard.

The name of the boat was Innisfallen and as it left Cork, it went down a channel past the locomotive sheds where I had been working. All my railway colleagues knew I was on the boat and all the whistles and hooters were blowing as we went past.

It was really touching, and I don't mind admitting I had tears in my eyes.

Frank pictured with Dublin lad Fred Kearns during his early days in England with West Ham.

EVENTS OF 1948

Britain's railways were nationalised.

Mohandas Karamchand (Mahatma) Gandhi was assassinated.

Prince Charles was born.

The game of Scrabble was launched.

The Olympic Games were held in London.

Frank O'Farrell joined West Ham United.

2

EAST END TO NORTH END

Bow bells strike, another night
Your eyes are heavy and your limbs all ache,
You've bought some coffee, butter and bread,
You can't make a thing 'cause the meat is dead,
You've moved away ...

David Bowie

WE LANDED in Fishguard in Wales and travelled up by train to Paddington. It was my first time out of Ireland and London, after Cork, frightened me a little. But I wasn't homesick and I went into digs with John and Tommy for about six months.

It was a bit crowded, we had two single beds and a camp bed in our room and I slept on the camp bed. The husband, wife and daughter of the house had their own rooms. It shouldn't really have been three in a room but we were all from Cork so we could adapt. Tommy would like a drink at the weekends, so it was a bit lonely at times, but Sundays were OK because I went to St Anthony's Church. They would have a dance at their social club on Sunday evenings. To me, the East End was not as rough as people would have you believe. I met some very nice people, and in due course, my wife too.

Once I had got a feel for the place, I left Tommy and Johnny and I went and stayed with a lovely Cockney couple, Mr and Mrs Davey, at 4 Nigel Road in Forest Gate. Mr Davey was a cooper (a barrel-maker) with the Esso company, and a big West Ham fan. He would talk football all evening with me. Sometimes I wanted to read, but he always wanted to talk about the team and the game. I stayed with the Daveys for six years until I got married in 1954.

As well as going to the cinema and theatre a lot, at weekends

I'd also explore London. I used to go to Hyde Park after Mass and listen to the soapbox speakers. Mr and Mrs Davey were in the Co-operative Labour Party and their local MP, Percy Daines, arranged for me to visit the Houses of Parliament. I got about six or seven players to come as well which was quite an achievement. We were taken up Big Ben and shown the woolsack.

I went to night classes to learn woodwork in the winter - no-one there knew I was footballer - and I was also asked to join a church group, called the Legion of Mary, by a Scottish lad named Eddie Smith. He formed a group down in the parish of St Michael's in East Ham and this is where I first met my wife Ann.

I went down for a meeting and Ann and her sister were there. After a couple of meetings I thought about asking her out as she was such a nice girl. But then I went missing for a few weeks as my own centre-half crashed into my face during a reserve game and my right eyelid was left hanging off. I had five stitches in the wound and was taken to London Hospital at Whitechapel and spent a couple of days there.

I was unconscious at first and after they'd stitched me up they kept me in over the weekend to assess the damage done to the cheekbones and my eye. All the other men in the ward thought I was a drunken Irishman who had been in a fight!

Apparently Ann (her surname was Sheridan like the film-star of the time) had said to someone at the group that I was a nice gentleman and did they know why had I stopped going to the meetings? I went back and asked her out and we courted for about three years before marrying.

Ann was the youngest of three children - she had an older brother George (now deceased) and a sister, Maureen. Ann was a secretary at Unilever and she asked me what I did. I replied that I played football, and she thought I was talking about my hobby. She didn't know people played football for a living, which I found quite funny. Her father, an Irish merchant seaman from Waterford, had died when she was only seven. Her mum was a Cockney and suffered from poor health. They had experienced the blitz during the War and Ann once told me a sad story of when there were six coffins in the church one Sunday morning after a whole family had been killed in an air-raid.

Although Ann's not Irish, she is from Irish descent and a

Frank at West Ham United.

practising Catholic - so we had shared values and interests from the start.

They had a good supporters' club at West Ham and once a month they'd have a social evening and dancing. We would go and meet the others players' girlfriends and wives. There was nothing like WAGS in those days though. Ann knew John Dick's wife, Sue, as her sister, Beryl, had been in the same year as Ann at East Ham Grammar School for Girls. It was Ann and I who introduced John and Sue at one of the West Ham dances. Ann still keeps in touch with two other of her school-mates, Pamela Purdom (née Gowan) and Peggy Bryant (née Norman).

The parish priest, Father Cahill, asked the Legion of Mary group to do a census of the parish for him, which meant knocking on doors and asking if people living there were Catholics. We were dismissed with rude remarks at times, while one time when I said to the lady who answered the door that we were taking a census for the Catholic parish, she said "Are they Labour or Conservative?"

One night I knocked at a door and this woman said "I know you - you're Frank O'Farrell and play for West Ham reserves." She and her husband were huge fans and watched all the teams play,

Frank with West Ham team-mates Malcolm Allison and Jim Barrett.

reserves and the A team as well, and she invited us in. They had a budgie in a cage and her husband said "What's your name?" The budgie said "Peter Nelson, 141 Clements Road, East Ham E6 - up the 'Ammers!" Mr Nelson had taught him to say that.

It was my first taste of being recognised as a footballer in England. I told her we were doing a census for our church and she said she was a Catholic, but not practising. Before leaving I asked her to think about attending Mass again. She said she would if I got in the first team, and she kept her promise. She started coming to Mass and I believe her husband started coming as well. Whether Peter came or not is not recorded! So getting into the West Ham first team had started me off doing some good work for the Lord.

I've always had the philosophy that I had to do a bit more as the Good Lord had been good to me. I had my ups and downs like everyone else but he did me three favours. I could have died three times in my life (I will elaborate on the other two occasions later in the book) so whenever I had time I always tried to do a little work for the church.

I found the training at West Ham hard, but the atmosphere around the club was good. The War hadn't long finished and some of the players had been involved so there was a lot of banter about their experiences. Sometimes you had to wonder how they'd ever won the War when you heard of these fellows' contribution to it!

Goalkeeper Ernie Gregory told us a story about when he worked on a searchlight station on Wanstead Flats. One night they picked out a German bomber and the sergeant said "Put that blooming light out - he's seen us". That's what they were supposed to do - spotlight them!

I found it very hard to understand some of the Cockneys and they found it hard to understand me with my broad Irish accent. So I had to modify it a little to be understood.

The West Ham manager was Charlie Paynter, a dapper man who had been at the club since 1932. He always wore a bow tie with a pin in it, and had plenty of authority. He wasn't into the tactics of the game but he was very well respected.

He was like a father figure really. He didn't interfere much and though I didn't play in the first team under him, I did go away with the team on a couple of occasions and he'd say a few words in the dressing room before the match and again at half-time.

West Ham weren't a limited company back then, but owned by the Cearns family and the Pratt family. Both families were nice, and always very helpful.

I settled in quite well, and was playing for the A team in the Eastern Counties League. I would also play for the reserves in the Football Combination but I didn't break into the first team for a couple of years.

There were probably about 45 professionals - they had three teams at the time and clubs had bigger staffs then due to the maximum wage rule. There was still rationing after the War and they used to give us a free lunch at a place called the Denmark Hotel. It was about half a mile from the ground and we'd either walk there or get the bus.

Chocolate wasn't rationed in Ireland so when I went home I always used to bring some back for my landlady, or some other stuff not rationed in Ireland, and she'd be delighted. Sometimes I might come back wearing a nice sports coat and one of the players would ask me to sell it to him as there was also clothes rationing in England.

During pre-season we'd train twice a day, but during the season it was usually training in the mornings and then it was off to the cinema in the afternoon. It was good meeting other people and getting used to their accents. One of the top opera companies came down to the East End every year, to the People's Palace on the Mile End Road, and Johnny McGowan and me used to go to a couple of shows. We both liked opera.

I didn't drink but some of the other players would at the weekend - they'd have a good time and then come and sweat it off on the Monday.

For training, we would wear spikes if we were doing sprinting, or plimsolls or boots if we were having a practice match. We would wear a heavy sweater in the winter, and sometimes the drinkers would put two sweaters on to sweat more off. We did a lot of running, with perhaps a practice match on the Tuesday, but we didn't see a lot of the ball. Things started to develop on that later on with Ted Fenton.

The trainer was a man called Billy Moore. He used to supervise all the training - and he liked a fag! He was the physiotherapist as well though he never smoked when he was treating your injuries.

The training was mostly running. We didn't have any training facilities at Upton Park - if the pitch was wet you couldn't go on it - but there was a little plot of wasteland behind the stand and we trained there. The remains of Green Street House, which was known as Anne Boleyn's castle, were on the boundary of this piece of land and remained there until Upton Park was developed years later.

Though the training was hard, it was nothing compared to shovelling coal and there was a genuine warmth among the players. I can honestly say that I never made any enemies.

I got on really well with Billy Moore. He was much older than me and had played in the famous White Horse FA Cup final of 1923 for West Ham. Billy played outside-right in the final against Bolton Wanderers, and Jimmy Ruffell played outside-left. Too many spectators, about 120,000, were let into the stadium - there were no all-ticket matches back then - and the policeman on the

Frank (right) in discussion with West Ham manager Ted Fenton, coach Billy Moore and goalkeeper Ernie Gregory.

The West Ham United staff in 1949-50. Back (left to right): R.Watts, D.Howe, P.Peters, D.Woodards (groundsman), T. Williamson, Eric Parsons, Ernie Devlin, Johnny McGowan, Moroney, Wally St Pier (assistant trainer), Charlie Paynter junior. Third row: Billy Moore K.Bradly, Dick Walker, Norman 'Norrie' Corbett, Fred Kearns, Derek Parker, Bill Stephens, (director), Jim Barrett, Terry Woodgate, Almer Hall, Danny McGowan, Bill Robinson, Bainbridge, LC Cearns (director), Charlie Paynter (manager) Sitting at front: W.Richards,

Ernie Gregory, George Taylor, Eric Armstrong, John Ballantyne. Second row:
Ron Wilson, Ken Wright, Steve Forde, Jack Yeomanson, Frank O'Farrell, Tommy
(trainer), Ted Fenton (assistant manager), J.Gibson, Eddie Chapman, Ron Cater,
H.Butler (assistant trainer), JE Johnson. Front row: FH Cearns (secretary), AC Davis
WJ Cearns (chairman), Ken Tucker, Gerry Gazzard, Jackie Wood, Don Wade, Ken
Andy Malcolm, D.Rawkins, Alfie Noakes, G.Gatward.

famous white horse wasn't able to prevent the crowd encroaching onto the pitch. Billy used to say that West Ham were not able to use their wingers because the crowd was too close to the pitch, and it was felt to be one of their strengths. He reckoned it was why West Ham lost the final 2-0.

Charlie Paynter's retirement was the beginning of my first-team career. I was getting to the stage where I felt I was ready for the first team. Tommy Moroney was still the star man, and Tommy and Norman Corbett were keeping me out of the team.

Tommy played both left and right-half, and inside-forward. I was always considered a left-half, even though I played on the right once or twice. I was always happier on the left as I was a natural left-footer.

I was a trier, and always willing to learn, and I thought I was playing well enough to be in the first team so I went up to Charlie Paynter's office to have a chat with him. It was up a long flight of stairs so I was knackered and nervous by the time I got up there. I knocked on his door. "Come in - hello Frank, sit down, what can I do for you?" "I think I've been playing well enough to play in the first team." "I think you haven't enough experience," was his reply.

They were celebrating the Battle of Britain at the time, hailing the young pilots who had driven back the Germans and prevented an invasion. I said "they got their experience in the cockpit and I will only get experience if you put me in the first team." I thought it was a good argument and I put my point over. I had learned to put my case better than I had when I didn't fancy cleaning that filthy steam engine back in Ireland! Charlie didn't have an answer - he just said you have made a good point and leave it with me. But it was only when Charlie decided to retire that I actually got my chance in the first team.

Ted Fenton, who had played for West Ham and had been manager at Colchester United, was appointed to succeed Charlie.

My first-team debut actually came in November 1950 in Charlie's testimonial game at Upton Park against Arsenal, who had won the FA Cup the previous season. I had gone along just to watch the match, having had my tea, a marvellous meal of Irish stew, at my digs. Then all of a sudden I was playing.

Tommy Moroney and some other players were injured and I

was the only wing-half they had. I had no time to worry about making my debut, which was probably a good thing, and I was thrown in at the deep end against an Arsenal side who had some great players.

I was up against a player called Reg Lewis and I felt I had a good game. It probably helped I didn't have time to think about the game, or be too nervous. I was inside the gate and then

Signing autographs for young West Ham fans. They are taking particular interest in the 'new' ballpoint pen.

suddenly I was playing - I can't remember who told me but it was one of the staff looking for me.

It was an evening match under floodlights - we had lights early at West Ham - and I had already played in some friendlies under them.

I was told I had a good game but I didn't really believe it until the team-sheet went up for the next match. I kept my place for the trip to Notts County, who had Tommy Lawton playing at centre-forward. I had been waiting two years for my chance, and now I had it and I was pleased with my early performances, even though we were beaten 4-1 at Meadow Lane.

You had to wait until the Friday before the game before the team-sheet was posted up on the back of the dressing-room door. Usually I would look at the sheet and see I wasn't there and in the reserves instead, but now I was in the first team and I couldn't quite believe it.

I stayed in the team for the rest of the season, more or less, and I felt I had finally made it, though I don't know what I'd have

West Ham United in 1955-56. Back (left to right): Dave Sexton, John Bond, Ernie Gregory, Malcolm Allison, Noel Cantwell, Frank O'Farrell. Front (left to right): Malcolm Musgrove, Harry Hooper, Billy Dare, John Dick, Ken Tucker.

done if I hadn't succeeded as a footballer. I don't think I could have gone back to shovelling coal.

Ted Fenton had a different attitude to Charlie, who was far more cautious on things like this. Ted didn't worry about putting me in the team. There was a new breed of manager coming into the game and Ted was one of them. He talked and listened to players and his attitude was more forward-thinking. He was a lot younger than Charlie too, and when you are young you tend to make braver decisions.

There were changes in training too. We'd be having a practice match and Ted would stop the match and say things like "Frank you're in the wrong position just watch out for his creeping behind your back and keep your eye on the ball." He would teach you things. With Charlie, there were few tactics. He'd just pick the team and say go out and play.

At the time, centre-half Dick Walker was club captain, and a good captain too. He was an ex-paratrooper who had been parachuted into Crete during the war. He was a big handsome man, a Cockney from Dagenham with a lovely personality. He said things that coming from other people might have been offensive. But the way he said it made it OK. He helped me a lot when I was in the reserves.

Ken Tucker, the outside-left, was a flamboyant character who also had his own shop on the Barking Road, just around the corner from the ground, and always had a wad of banknotes in his pocket. He was well known for back-heeling the ball, often when you weren't expecting it.

Ernie Gregory was the first-choice goalkeeper, a big chap who had also been in the army, while another of the wing-halves was Derek Parker, a very mobile player and a good passer of the ball who played for England B, going on tour with them to Australia. He could run all day.

I met up with Derek again in recent years in bizarre circumstances. My daughter in Colchester had a plumber doing some work at her house and he saw my picture and said "Oh my father played football." He was Derek Parker's son and they arranged for us to get together the next time I went up there. We enjoyed a couple of hours reminiscing. Sadly he has since passed away.

Harry Hooper was an excellent outside-right who came to the club with his father, Harry senior, from the north-east. His father had played for Sheffield United and Harry was a bright young fellow who was a great crosser of the ball and could score a goal or two as well. Eventually he was transferred to Wolverhampton Wanderers for a big fee, £25,000 I think.

Jimmy Andrews was a small Scot who played on the wing. Like me he also went into management and when I went to Cardiff City in 1973 I took him as my coach. He then took over as manager at Ninian Park when I left to go to Iran.

John Bond was one of the younger players, a right-back from Colchester. John was a lovely striker of the ball but wasn't the best tackler and didn't like heading the ball. But with Noel Cantwell, they made a pair of good full-backs, with Malcolm Allison at centre-half for a while until Ken Brown came in. Malcolm was diagnosed with tuberculosis and that effectively ended his playing career in 1957.

Later I took John and Ken to Torquay when I became manager there and they both did well for me. They were experienced players and I knew what they were about.

Norman Corbett was a right-half who had been at West Ham since before the War so he was something of a veteran when I got there. He kept his place at right-half for a while and I think it was Derek Parker who succeeded him. Billy Dare was a centre-forward who came from Brentford. He was small for a centre-forward, but he knew where the net was.

John Dick was a very good player, and once netted a hat-trick in an FA Cup Sixth Round tie at Tottenham in 1956. We were 3-0 up at half-time but they battled back to draw 3-3. We made a few errors, like John Bond going upfield and losing the ball for their first goal, that sparked them into action. They beat us 2-1 in the replay at Upton Park, but lost to Manchester City in the semi-final. It was disappointing to lose the replay as we had been playing well and fancied our chances of reaching Wembley. As a player, it was the nearest I got to the FA Cup final.

Mike Grice came from Colchester as well, a right-winger who arrived at the club just as I was leaving. And Billy Lansdowne was a wing-half but he was behind me, younger than me, and he got into the team after I left.

Andy Malcolm was a good, hard-tackling right-half who I think eventually went to Chelsea, while Eric Parsons was a right-winger who lived down in Eastbourne and used to travel up every day by train. We called him 'Rabbit' as he used to run like one, and he too was transferred to Chelsea.

Dave Sexton was a nice lad, and a versatile player who was very intelligent. He had been educated by the Jesuits up in Stamford Hill. His father, Archie, had been a professional boxer.

We would travel up to Grange Farm in Chigwell for pre-season training on the bus, but Dave always came on the train. He always used to pick up The Daily Telegraph at the station, and make up a news quiz at lunchtime for us. We would split into two teams and it was a lot of fun, especially when John Dick used to say things like "Who cares about the Secretary of State?" He would rather bet on two flies going up the wall! He was a lively lad and a very fine player, and I liked him a lot.

Bobby Moore was also on the ground staff, though I never saw him develop as he broke into the team after I left the club. But I was aware of him being there as a ground staff boy.

I always got on well with Malcolm Musgrove, and that lasted for all my career. We were good friends from the start. He was a very direct winger, quite strong, could cross a ball with both feet, and scored the odd goal or two as well.

He was one of the new breed of footballers who would talk about the game. We were always encouraged to talk football, and the likes of Dave Sexton and Malcolm Allison went to a local cafe, Cassettari's, on the Barking Road, along with the rest of us, after training and we'd be moving the salt cellars, tea cups and spoons around as we talked tactics. Everybody would have their say and we would have some deep discussions, even arguments, on how the game was going. I had been made captain and I made my views known.

West Ham were one of the first clubs where players got together to talk and discuss the game, and then put some of our ideas into action. Ted Fenton had the same sort of philosophy as us and he took notice of what we were trying to do and encouraged us.

The continentals were starting to make a major impact on the game. Whereas English football was direct, with two fast wingers crossing from the flanks, the continentals had a short passing build-up, and then the Hungarians introduced the withdrawn centre-forward, an innovation that we would analyse and see how beneficial it could be to us.

We also went on coaching courses run by Walter Winterbottom, the England manager. He was a great thinker about the game and people listened to him. He was very influential on the development of the game. You also met players and coaches from other clubs on these courses and that was also beneficial.

Most of the cafe talk at West Ham was inspired by Malcolm Allison. He had a good influence on the club, though his failing was that he didn't always win people over. He tended to be too dogmatic and he'd say things like "he can't effing play" and "that's a load of rubbish."

I particularly recall one team talk with Ted Fenton involving a Cockney lad called Alfie Noakes. He didn't play in the first team, mainly the reserves, but he'd talk about things and was a bright little fellow. Ted would ask for ideas and Alfie, who couldn't pronounce his ths, said "I fink we should do some weight training." It was a fair point but Malcolm rubbished it.

"Effing weight training, what are you on about?" That was

John Bond, Malcolm Allison, John Dick and Frank after a sea water bath at Hove as West Ham prepare for an FA Cup tie against Blackburn Rovers in 1956.

Malcolm all over - he had strong opinions and he expressed them. Alfie argued his case, saying "Well I fink they'd be good 'cos them wrestlers are strong and we could be stronger players and fitter by doing weight training." Later Malcolm became a big fan of weights - we'd get the weights in the gym and do circuit training yet when the idea first came from young Alfie, he had rubbished it without a second thought. That was Malcolm's failing. He didn't always put his case over reasonably and tended to dismiss anyone who had different views to his own. He was very impulsive.

Malcolm had done his national service in Austria and he saw how they played out there. It was different and he picked up some good points. He, like many of us, had been influenced when he watched Hungary beat England 6-3 at Wembley in 1953.

He wanted to develop the game and he had good ideas and people went along with him. Ted Fenton went along with it but Ted let Malcolm take on too much and in the end it lessened his own authority. Ted had introduced his own innovations like lightweight continental boots instead of those heavy, hard toe-capped boots you had to soak in hot water to soften them.

Malcolm said we should get lighter kit - we used to play in really heavy shirts. West Ham were at the forefront of those quite radical changes and after I had left to go to Preston, I went over to see the Hammers play at Blackburn and they came out to warm up in beige tracksuits, which impressed the Preston players who were with me.

I also remember Malcolm saying at one stage that we didn't need to play with shin pads. He felt they were too heavy and as a player, you needed to be light. He chose to experiment without them against Birmingham City - he was the only player not wearing them - and he went into an early tackle with a centre-forward called Cyril Trigg. He got a big gash down his shin, and he reverted to wearing shin pads again after that!

Noel Cantwell came from Cork like me and I'd played junior football with his older brother Frank. He was known as 'Skippy', a little lad at that time, and Tommy Moroney recommended him to West Ham. He later went to Manchester United and led them to FA Cup success in 1963, and became a manager of course, with Coventry City and Peterborough United.

Grange Farm, where we trained, was way out and we'd stay

out there all day. They had good pitches and changing rooms whereas we had no training facilities like that at Upton Park. We'd do long cross-country runs through the Essex countryside, but also we'd do a lot of ball work and exercises too.

I liked training and it was never a problem for me. I depended on my energy levels as a wing-half going up and down the pitch. Training was never a bind.

Before matches we always used to have fillet steak, which is different to the eating habits in today's game. We'd have a nice juicy steak two or three hours before the game, though no chips with it, and then perhaps a bit of custard or milk pudding.

Being a Catholic, I wasn't allowed to eat meat on a Friday, which was a day of fast and abstinence then, and it sometimes complicated things when we were away and staying at hotels. They often had a set meal booked in advance, probably steak or chops, and I always had to stand up and say I don't eat meat on Fridays.

I was never afraid to make my point and it helped me as well in my career. If you believe in something, you shouldn't keep it to yourself. It was important to me, though I'd sometimes get a bit of ribbing from my team-mates.

It was like when I went to Holy Communion on Sundays when I was in digs. My landlady didn't understand it at all, but it is something I have always done. If you were going to Holy Communion at Mass, you had to fast from midnight and have your breakfast when you got home after Mass.

If we were playing at home, we'd have to report at a certain time and we'd have a team talk. We never warmed up on the pitch like today - we just got warmed up in the dressing room and then went out and played.

There were so many players on the staff at West Ham that we shared two dressing rooms. But it was a real homely club, and that environment came from the top.

The chairman, Mr WJ Cearns, sometimes used to come in the dressing rooms just to say "hello boys". When he died, we all lined up outside the ground as the cortege went past. His brother Frank was the secretary and later the Pratt family came in and they made you equally welcome. But it was always a prudent club and they never threw money around.

For away games, we would either go by coach or train. It would be by coach if it was within easy travelling distance, but for the long hauls to Lancashire and beyond, we would go on the train from King's Cross or St Pancras on the Friday.

Once when he played Cardiff City, the Cardiff fans planted a leek in the centre circle, and then in another game against Blackpool in the FA Cup, the fans paraded a duck around the ground before the kick-off. Supporters did those sort of things then and it was part of the fun of going to football.

Things were a lot different in the 1950s to what they are these days. In an FA Cup tie against Blackpool at Upton Park, I scored the second goal to put us 2-0 up. As I ran back for the kick-off, Blackpool's Stan Mortensen said to me "Well done, Frank, you'll feel better now as two is better than one." It was very generous of him, and not the sort of thing that happens these days. It was a different era with totally different attitudes.

We played in front of some big crowds and I really enjoyed the atmosphere. The crowd didn't really bother me and I didn't get distracted. The fans weren't all tanked up with beer, a lot of them had their children with them, and you could take your family in safety.

The first match that Ann came to was a 6-0 home defeat by Sheffield Wednesday in December 1951. We got slaughtered and

Frank in action for the Hammers against Liverpool at Anfield.

I wouldn't allow her to come anymore as I said she was a jinx! We had only been courting a few months. She wasn't really a football fan so she wasn't too bothered. She used to stay at home after that and say prayers for us.

Derek Dooley played for Sheffield Wednesday that day, and people will remember that he later lost his leg after a collision in a game against Preston North End.

After her father had died when she was seven, there was little football talk in Ann's house and she didn't know much about the game. Even though she did not attend West Ham matches, I did take her to Chelsea once, and she came out with the line about "the two pretty flags the men are waving up and down." They were of course the linesmen!

I recall before an FA Cup tie at Sheffield United, we went to the theatre the night before to see Harry Secombe. I was always a fan of his, and he was brilliant. He knew we were in the audience and made some cracks about Swansea winning the cup. The club often used to pay for us to go to the theatre or cinema on Friday nights before away games.

We stayed at some top hotels and there were always autograph hunters around. There was one, a little Jewish boy at West Ham who I'd often see when I'd come out after training. I was wearing a sacred heart religious badge on my coat at the time and his friend said "What's that badge you're wearing on your coat Mr O'Farrell?" The little Jewish boy said "That's because he's a Catholic - that's the greatest religion in the world." I met that lad about five years ago at West Ham and he was still collecting autographs - he must be about 60 now.

One of the best goals I ever scored was at home to Liverpool in September 1956. Their goalkeeper was Tommy Younger, and I beat him with a left-foot volley. I caught it just right and it was a great goal. I met Tommy again after I went to Preston and he still talked about it then. I was playing well at West Ham and the press nicknamed me 'Tranquility Frank.'

I also remember making my first overseas trip with West Ham in 1952. I had never flown before, and never been anywhere except England but there had some big floods in Belgium and Holland. We went to Belgium to play a match to raise money to help the local people who had been affected.

Around this time I was also honoured by being selected to play for the Football Combination representative team against the Belgium Combination team in Brussels. The rest of the team was Ted Ditchburn (Spurs), John Hewie (Charlton Athletic), Joe Wade (Arsenal), Jimmy Scoular (Portsmouth), Ron Greenwood (Fulham), Peter Harris (Portsmouth), Peter Murphy (Birmingham City), Bedford Jezzard (Fulham), Tommy Harmer (Spurs) and Don Roper (Arsenal). The manager was Arthur Rowe of Tottenham.

I also made my international debut while I was at Upton Park. I was competing with Pat Saward of Aston Villa for a place in the Irish team, and I made my debut in 1952 in a 6-0 defeat by Austria in Vienna. It wasn't the best way to start, but we played them again at Dalymount Park the following year and I scored in a 4-0 win. I scored again in my next international as well, a 5-3 defeat by France.

Austria were a big team in those days, and had the impressive

The West Ham players about to board their coach at Letchworth Hall in Hertfordshire, where they often used to go to prepare for FA Cup ties.

Ernst Ocwirk in their side - they used to call him 'Clockwork' because he made things tick in midfield.

I won nine Irish caps in total and played under three different managers, Doug Livingstone, Alex Stevenson, a Liverpudlian who spent all his career with Everton, and the former Manchester United player Johnny Carey.

Some of the games were played on Sundays, so you would play on the Saturday as normal, then get the ferry from Liverpool to Dublin and play on the Sunday. I don't remember the preparation being anything special, just a bit of training, a talk and then we would go out and play the best we could. I think the fee for playing was £5 at the time.

On reflection, I am disappointed I didn't play in more than nine games for Ireland. Perhaps had I played for a more successful team than West Ham, I might have got picked more often, but I was always proud to pull on the green shirt, and my parents were proud too. I was also proud to be from Cork and playing for my country.

I was 29 when I moved to Preston North End in the 1956-57 season. Ted Fenton was trying to build a promotion team at West Ham and I didn't feel I was part of his plans, especially when he told me that Preston were interested in me. There were a few wing-halves at West Ham at that time, and I had been playing in the reserves a fair bit. I'd had a good game against Preston the previous season in the FA Cup and Cliff Britton, the Preston manager, had also watched me in a reserve match. Unlike these days, with the improved fitness, 29 was deemed as being quite old and I think Ted was looking to bring in younger players.

I knew Ted was after a centre-forward and he had enquired about Eddie Lewis at Preston, and Preston must have asked whether they could take me in a swap deal.

I went home and told Ann and she said "Where is Preston?" She'd never been outside London and I said it probably won't be up to much, and very smoggy like London. But when we got to Preston it was nice, not far from the coast at Blackpool, close to the Lake District and with some lovely countryside.

One problem about a possible move to Preston would be coming back to London at intervals to take our daughter Bernadette to the brilliant Great Ormond Street Hospital, where she had been under a wonderful surgeon by the name of Mr Innis Williams. Bernadette had some complications when she was born and used to have regular hospital visits for some years.

She was born on a Friday and I had to play the next day for West Ham against Plymouth. That was a difficult game for me as my head was full of anxieties about our new-born baby. I needed Cliff Britton to reassure me that he would allow me to travel to London from time to time when Bernadette had a hospital appointment.

Ann and I travelled up to Preston by train to meet Cliff. Just before boarding the train at Euston station, who should appear but Victor Railton, a sports reporter for the London Evening News. How he got hold of the news that I was travelling to Preston I will never know, but I guess that is what a good newsman is all about - finding out good stories.

Cliff met us at Preston station and took us to a hotel and one of his staff picked us up the following morning to take us to Deepdale to negotiate a possible transfer. While I was in talks, one of the staff, George Bargh, took Ann on a tour around Preston, pointing out the club houses that some players rented from the club, one of which would be allocated to me if I signed.

The negotiations went well, Cliff impressed me, and provided I got my accrued share of benefit from West Ham for the service I had given the club, and Ann liked the area after looking around, there was no reason why I would not want to join a club of Preston's stature. It would mean playing in the First Division alongside players like Tom Finney, Willie Cunningham, Tommy Docherty, Tommy Thompson, Sammy Taylor and Fred Else.

Ann and I would have to sell our house in East Ham, which we had bought for £1,750 on a mortgage when we got married and where we thought we would live for many years. We were married at St Antony's Franciscan church in Forest Gate in May 1954 by Father Dermot (Order of Friars Minor). The wedding was at the end of the season and quite a few players attended, as well as the West Ham chairman, Mr Pratt, and the manager, Ted Fenton.

An Irish tenor sang Ave Maria during the Mass and some of the players said it was the nicest thing they had ever heard.

It was a lovely day and my parents came over from Ireland. I'd already taken Ann home for a holiday in Cork and she got on well with my family. For the honeymoon, we caught the train from Paddington to Fishguard, and travelled on the Innisfallen to Cork where I hired a car and did a tour of Ireland, visiting Waterford, where Ann's late father had come from.

When Ann was expecting Bernadette, she developed diabetes. I had been away with West Ham playing in Sheffield and when I got home on the Saturday night, she was not well. She had fallen down the stairs on the Friday and subsequently she was diagnosed with diabetes. As there was no history of diabetes in Ann's family, the doctors told her the cause was probably due to the shock of her fall. She was taken into hospital on Christmas Eve, our first Christmas together, and she stayed in hospital until February when Bernadette was born. I think she is marvellous the way she has managed her diabetes. She has to inject four times every day - morning, teatime and two at bedtime - and is very disciplined.

Considering she has had diabetes for over 50 years, she's very well. It can be a quite serious and debilitating illness and I can see the signs when her blood sugar gets low. If she doesn't have something sweet to raise the blood sugar level, it gets worse and she could go into a coma. But she has always been a very strong character and has never drunk alcohol - and I think she is a model for anyone with diabetes.

Ann recently celebrated her 80th birthday, and I have the greatest admiration and love for her. Having diabetes and having to cope with my profession of playing football and then managing, and the ups and downs it has brought, cannot have been easy for her. She also had to cope with losing two babies at birth, Clare and Kieran. They are buried in Preston Cemetery and we still continue to visit their little graves once or twice a year when we are up that way.

In my negotiations with Cliff Britton, he agreed to facilitate me going to London from time to time when Bernadette had an appointment at Great Ormond Street. I signed for North End after Ted Fenton guaranteed he would pay me my accrued share of benefit for my service to West Ham, which was £500 tax free. Ted ummed and aahed a little when I telephoned him asking for the

£500, but I knew he wanted Eddie Lewis and would not get him if I did not sign for Preston, and he relented in the end. Funnily enough Eddie actually travelled down to London with us on the train when we went back, and I told him all about West Ham.

I went in digs in Preston for a while and looked around for a house and Ann stayed in London, organising the sale of our house. I shared some digs with Tommy Docherty for a few weeks before I was shown one of the club houses, a semi-detached in a place called Duchy Avenue in Fulwood. It was very nice with a garage, and only a ten-minute walk from the ground. I would walk to home games - and walk back - because I didn't have a car when I first got there. You'd meet a few fans as you were walking down and they'd wish you all the best and ask how things were going to go. You were a lot closer to the fans in those days. I feel players have distanced themselves from the fans today, and that's not a good thing.

The club said they would decorate the house for me, so we sold our house in London for about £2,500, making a bit of a

Helping out in defence during Preston's home game in the snow against Leeds United in 1957, and shielding goalkeeper Fred Else from the great John Charles.

profit, packed our bags and moved up to Preston just before Christmas in 1956.

We went to Preston open market that Christmas and to this day Ann said she has never tasted brussels sprouts like those she bought on that visit.

Preston manager Cliff Britton was a great figure of authority. He had played at a very high standard for Everton and England, and had managed in the First Division too with Everton. He could talk about the game, the tactics and so on and we'd put his ideas into practice during training.

He was older than Ted Fenton although he was of the same mindset. He was into tactics and he impressed on me not to get caught upfield during games.

I thought Cliff was very knowledgeable about the game. On Fridays before matches we'd go upstairs to a room and there'd be a table there with a blackboard on it and we'd have a tactical talk on how we were going to prepare. I was quite pleased he was like that as I'd had a bit of it at West Ham, though I would say he was a more authoritative figure than Ted Fenton.

Some of the players didn't like the fact that his word was final, and he was particularly strict on having no alcohol around. He had been brought up in the West Country with a Methodist background. Sometimes you'd play on a very hot day early in the season and they'd put a crate of beer down for us - but he wouldn't have it. He'd kick it straight out and he wouldn't buy an alcoholic drink for anyone. Tommy Docherty used to say that he would ban us from eating wine gums!

There wasn't a big drinking culture at West Ham or Preston, but back then there wasn't the sort of drinking culture that there is today. People might have had a drink but you wouldn't see young people drunk up to their eyeballs and behaving badly.

I have a drink now and then but if I don't, I don't miss it. If I am in company I'll have a glass of wine sometimes. I'm not hostile to drink, I'm only hostile to the drinks industry and the way they ply youngsters with cheap drink and all the problems it causes. Football has to ask itself whether it should be promoting the drinks industry by taking money in sponsorships.

Compared to West Ham, we played a much shorter passing game at Preston, and were nowhere near as direct. You had someone like Jimmy Baxter in midfield, with outstanding ability and a brain like a computer. He could see the pass and he could play a long ball or a short ball, and would play people through when he saw gaps.

My role was on the left-hand side of midfield, to trundle up and down between the two penalty areas, get my tackles in and sometimes go forward and get a shot in.

Preston had better players than West Ham and they were playing at a higher level in the First Division. I did what the manager wanted me to do, sometimes he would say I was going forward too much and leaving gaps behind so then I'd readjust my game. We had Tommy Docherty on the other side, and he tended to go forward more than me but had great powers of recovery and was very quick. I'd often cover for him when he went up the field.

The training was much the same as it was at West Ham, though Cliff Britton was probably more perceptive and he'd pick out things in more detail. We'd play five-a-side, practice matches and we'd practise free-kicks.

Preston North End in 1957-58. Back (left to right): Ken Waterhouse, Tommy Docherty, Willie Cunningham, Fred Else, Joe Dunn, Joe Walton, Jimmy Milne (trainer). Front (left to right): Les Dagger, Tommy Thompson, Tom Finney, Jimmy Baxter, Sam Taylor, Frank O'Farrell.

Of course Ann and I frequently travelled down to London with Bernadette and during the second or third season at Preston, I was told that Arsenal were interested in me. I thought to myself that it would be a good move, and would save the constant trek down to the hospital.

Somehow it got out in the press and that annoyed Cliff. I hadn't put it in the press but someone had got hold of the story. He called me in and said he wasn't happy it was in the papers. He said seeing as I wanted to leave the club he was not picking me on the following Saturday.

Instead I played against Barnsley reserves and I did my cartilage. I had to have an operation on my knee and though I played in the first team again, I didn't get the move to Arsenal. I went in for physiotherapy after the operation and Cliff said "Happy New Year." I thought I haven't got my move to Arsenal, I've done my cartilage and he's saying Happy New Year!

But generally, I have happy memories of my time at Preston. Everyone has setbacks in life, things like illnesses and the like, and you have to be able to cope with them. If you have a stable home life, and are a strong couple, you come through them.

The Preston trainer was Jimmy Milne, father of Gordon Milne. He was a Scot, very honest and open, and very forthright. He didn't beat about the bush and if you weren't playing well, he would tell you. There was never any guff. He was a good trainer and Cliff Britton was a good manager, though he was not liked by everyone.

Tom Finney played most of his career on the right-wing for Preston, but he became an even better player when he was turned into a centre-forward. A lot of people believe Cliff Britton was responsible for that move, but it was actually Jimmy Milne who played him at centre-forward before Cliff came to the club. Jimmy deserved the credit for that. Tom was a brilliant player and was devastating as a centre-forward. Bill Shankly used to say that Tom could play with his overcoat on and that the opposition would have two players marking him in the pre-match warm-up!

Finney and Stanley Matthews were both great players, and they were unplayable on their day down the wing. But Tom was also a goalscorer where Stan wasn't. Stan did all his work on the wing laying on the chances for others. Tom did that as well but then he'd come inside and rattle the ball into the back of the net. Full-backs often used to try and clog Tom, but he was never intimidated by them and would often end up making them look even bigger fools.

Tom was not only a fantastic player, but also a wonderful person. He was very modest and self-effacing. I can't speak highly enough of him as a person and he was one of those players who I never once heard use bad language.

He was called the 'Preston Plumber' and he'd come round and fix your tap washers or ballcock after training. We lived in houses that we rented from the club, and if there was a plumbing job to be done you'd ask Tom to come and have a look. Sometimes he wouldn't even take payment, even though he had his own plumbing business to run. He'd say it was all part of his life, playing football, training and doing his plumbing. And he was a top England international!

When we played against Stanley Matthews we used to try and not let him get hold of the ball. If he did, he would get to the goal-line and cut it back and then bang it's a chance. If he had a weakness, it was his left foot so we used to get him to cut inside using his left-foot if we could. But he was devastating if you let

Caricature by Bob Bond

him have the ball and he'd usually pick out his man, typically Stan Mortensen or Jackie Mudie.

I also played against Duncan Edwards. He was very mature for his age, and was playing in the First Division for Manchester United when he was only 16. He was a great player, and would surely have become a true giant in the game had he not been killed as a result of the Munich air crash in 1958.

Tommy Thompson was a great goalscorer, a 30 goal a season man, who had joined Preston from Aston Villa. He had a terrific shot and could always sniff out a chance and get his head to it. He had great awareness of what was happening around him. Tommy had originally played for Newcastle and was a Geordie lad. He is one of seven or eight players from that team still alive, and I look forward to seeing them when we have the chance to get together.

Tommy Docherty was a real bundle of energy. He refused to be beaten and was definitely a great player to have on your side.

We had quite a few Scots in the team, and Willie Cunningham was another of them. He was a lovely chap, and although he could be dour at times, he was as honest as the day is long. He played right-back, though he was naturally left footed. He wasn't quick but he timed his tackles perfectly. Willie also played for Scotland in the 1954 World Cup in Switzerland alongside Tommy Docherty.

Frank in action for Preston in their 3-1 win at Everton in the successful 1957-58 campaign.

The Preston party, with Frank fourth from the right, about to board their plane for the tour to Denmark and Sweden in 1957.

They used to tell a story about Willie and Frank Hill, the manager before Cliff Britton. During a team talk, Frank was suggesting to Willie what he should have been doing better with some aspect of his play. He then made the fatal mistake of asking Willie what he thought, and apparently Willie replied "I think you are talking ****!" I would love to have been present to witness that confrontation.

Fred Else was the Preston goalkeeper at the time and I think he later toured Australia with an England representative team.

They were decent guys and I got on with them all. I settled in well and I feel they respected me as they needed a left-half and I came in and had a good run. Just like at West Ham, I also acted as captain at times when Tom Finney wasn't playing.

We sometimes trained a couple of miles outside Preston at a place called Willow Farm. It was out in the country and we did our pre-season training there, but they also had a training ground next to Deepdale which we'd use during the week and for practice matches. It has since been turned into a car park. The training was similar to that at West Ham. Cliff Britton would probably go into a bit more detail and he'd supervise us as well.

Gordon Milne and Peter Thompson, who both went on to have great careers in the game, were youngsters at the club at the time. Preston had a decent youth policy, a bit like West Ham, and Gordon got into the side after Tommy Docherty was transferred to Arsenal. Sadly when things got tight they had to sell both Gordon and Peter.

I think Preston were always short of money and I suspect that was one of Cliff's problems. That and the fact the team was getting old. Tom Finney was coming towards the end of his career, and he started missing games through injury.

Tom could have gone to Italy for a lot of money earlier in his career, but Nat Buck, the Preston chairman, apparently told him that if he wasn't playing for Preston then he wasn't going to play for anyone. That was the way it was in those days.

My Preston debut was against Manchester City - my first game in Division One - and I scored in a 3-1 win. I hit a shot from outside the box with my left foot. It went in the corner and I was delighted. The other players were delighted for me too.

We didn't lose in the first 17 games I played so I was really happy with the way I had fitted in to the team. We finally finished third behind Manchester United and Tottenham.

The following season we were runners-up in the League, finishing five points behind champions Wolverhampton Wanderers. We produced some terrific performances and we were confident we had a team good enough to land the title.

But Cliff Britton didn't have the resources of clubs like Manchester United, Everton and Liverpool, and maybe if we had been able to strengthen the team, we might have been champions. The big clubs were all getting 50,000 crowds and we were getting 25,000 or so.

We had some great results that season, and one that stands out was an 8-0 hammering of Birmingham City in February in which both Tommy Thompson and Sammy Taylor scored hat-tricks, and Tom Finney netted twice.

Ray Shaw was the trainer at Birmingham at the time and later when I became Leicester manager, he was the chief scout there. He told me the story of when he got back to Birmingham after that 8-0 defeat at Deepdale, there were some fans at the railway station and they asked him what had happened. Gil Merrick was in goal

SEASON TO REMEMBER 1957-58

PRESTON NORTH END, RUNNERS-UP IN THE FOOTBALL LEAGUE

DIVISION ONE

Date	Opponent	Score	Scorers	Attendance
Aug 24	Nottingham Forest (a)	1-2	Taylor	33,285
Aug 27	Burnley (a)	0-2		27,804
Aug 31	Portsmouth (h)	4-0	Thompson 2, Finney, Baxter	24,422
Sept 4	Burnley (h)	2-1	Thompson, Finney	31,267
Sept 7	West Brom (a)	1-4	Docherty	29,768
Sept 11	Manchester City (a)	0-2		24,439
Sept 14	Tottenham Hotspur (h)	3-1	Thompson 2, Mayers	23,364
Sept 18	Manchester City (h)	6-1	Taylor 2, Finney 2, Thompson, Dagger	22,034
Sept 21	Birmingham City (a)	1-3	Thompson	24,894
Sept 28	Chelsea (h)	5-2	Taylor 3 (1 pen), Thompson, Finney	17,944
Oct 5	Newcastle United (a)	2-0	Taylor, Finney	36,131
Oct 12	Luton Town (h)	1-0	Finney (pen)	25,403
Oct 19	Sunderland (a)	0-0		34,676
Oct 26	Everton (h)	3-1	Mayers 2, Finney	31,449
Nov 2	Leeds United (a)	3-2	Mayers, Baxter (pen), Alston	23,832
Nov 9	Manchester United (h)	1-1	Finney	39,066
Nov 16	Leicester City (a)	3-1	Thompson, Finney, Taylor	27,319
Nov 23	Bolton Wanderers (h)	3-0	Thompson, Finney, Stevens og	28,036
Nov 30	Aston Villa (a)	2-2	Thompson, Taylor	25,847
Dec 7	Wolverhampton W. (h)	1-2	Hatsell	22,771
Dec 14	Arsenal (a)	2-4	Mayers, Thompson	31,840
Dec 21	Nottingham Forest (h)	2-0	Thompson, Mayers	20,945
Dec 25	Sheffield Wed. (a)	4-4	Thompson 2, Finney 2	25,525
Dec 26	Sheffield Wed. (h)	3-0	Thompson 2, Finney	28,053
Dec 28	Portsmouth (a)	2-0	Thompson, Mayers	31,735
Jan 11	West Brom (h)	3-1	Thompson, Finney (pen), Farrall	25,262
Jan 18	Tottenham Hotspur (a)	3-3	Thompson 2, Ryden og	43,941
Feb 1	Birmingham City (h)	8-0	Thompson 3, Taylor 3, Finney 2	21,511
Feb 8	Chelsea (a)	2-0	Thompson, Finney	42,704
Feb 22	Luton Town (a)	3-1	Thompson, Finney (pen), Taylor	22,549
Mar 1	Sunderland (h)	3-0	Thompson 2, Baxter	23,974
Mar 8	Everton (a)	2-4	Finney (pen), Baxter	43,291
Mar 15	Leeds United (h)	3-0	Finney 2, Thompson	21,353
Mar 19	Newcastle United (h)	2-1	Finney 2	24,787
Mar 29	Leicester City (h)	4-1	Thompson 2, Mayers, Finney	18,392
Apr 4	Blackpool (a)	2-1	Mayers, Baxter	29,029
Apr 5	Manchester United (a)	0-0		48,413
Apr 7	Blackpool (h)	2-1	Thompson, Taylor	32,626
Apr 12	Aston Villa (h)	1-1	Mayers	21,053
Apr 19	Wolverhampton W. (a)	0-2		46,001
Apr 21	Bolton Wanderers (a)	4-0	Hatsell 2, Thompson, Finney (pen)	24,067
Apr 26	Arsenal (h)	3-0	Mayers 2, Thompson	21,538

FA CUP

Date	Opponent	Score	Scorers	Attendance
Jan 4	Bolton Wanderers (h)	0-3		32,641

for them that day and they thought that Gil must have been injured or something like that. It was just one of those days when everything went right for us.

We scored 100 League goals that season, won 18 of our 21 home matches and only suffered two defeats in our last 21 matches, home and away. But we lost both fixtures against Wolves and those defeats proved decisive in the end.

During the 1956-57 season, I'd been complaining about a cold and one day we were doing some running around the track and my nose started to bleed. I went in the dressing room and Jimmy Milne tried to stop it with a cold compress, but it kept bleeding so he said they'd better take me down to Preston Royal Infirmary.

We went to casualty and they put plugs up my nose and I just sat there waiting. It was something called an epistaxis, and it carried on bleeding so they took me in and I think I was in there for a couple of weeks because they couldn't stop it. They were

Taking in the sights while on tour with Preston North End in South Africa in 1958. Pictured are (left to right) Tommy Thompson, Willie Cunningham, Frank and Harry Mattinson.

plugging me and injecting me, and they had to do a blood transfusion as I lost four pints of blood. You only have around eight pints of blood in your body and I'd lost half of mine, which was quite serious. They gave me a clotting agent to try and stop the bleeding.

A couple of players popped in to see me but I didn't realise how ill I really was until Father Bacon from the Jesuit church in Preston came in to give me the last rites, because if I'd kept bleeding I would have bled to death.

As quickly as they were giving me blood, I was losing it again - all from my nose. Eventually they gave me an injection - vitamin K I think it was - and thankfully that sort of kicked in and it stopped. I was in there for a while to get my blood levels back up again, and it was a worrying time. I was in a really bad way and it was a frightening experience.

I also had a little operation and they found a blood vessel that was either damaged or weak. It's like if you cut your hand and it heals the skin there is tougher than the rest and so they scarred the blood vessel and that made it stronger - that was the theory anyway. I didn't play for a few weeks after that, but I soon got back into the team.

What I remember, apart from the fact I wasn't well, was the nursing sister, Sister Hitchens, looking after me really well and giving me extra helpings of cheese souffle!

I went on a few end-of-season tours with Preston. Teams touring at the end of the season was quite common back then. They were a treat for doing well and we went to both Scandinavia and South Africa. The trip to South Africa was especially memorable and we saw Table Mountain in Cape Town, and visited the copper mines in Rhodesia.

I stayed at Preston for five years, but after I'd had a cartilage operation I was playing fewer games and the team was getting a little old. I was not expecting to be retained when the team finished bottom of Division One and were relegated at the end of the 1960-61 season, and that's exactly what happened.

But I left on good terms and really enjoyed my years at Deepdale. I am a member of the Preston North End Former Players Association and always try to get up for their annual dinner, when I meet up with a lot of my old colleagues.

EVENTS OF 1961

The farthing coin ceased to be legal tender.

The construction of the Berlin Wall began.

Barak Obama was born.

Yuri Gagarin became the first human to journey into outer space.

Tottenham Hotspur won the League and FA Cup double.

Frank O'Farrell became player-manager of Weymouth.

3

WISH YOU WERE HERE

Oh I do like to be beside the seaside,
I do like to be beside the sea,
I do like to stroll upon the prom, prom, prom,
Where the brass bands play
'Tiddely-om-pom-pom!'

John A.Glover-Kind

I WAS in my early 30s now and I began to think about life after playing football. I got to know a fellow Irishman and ex-Everton player called Peter Corr and he had a shop, and asked me to go into partnership with him. It was a newsagent's shop in Preston down by the docks and I agreed to become his partner. But it didn't work out as you'd have to get up really early in the morning for the papers and that didn't fit in with my routine. Peter (who was the uncle of the Irish musical group The Corrs) did most of the early starts but sometimes he'd sit back and I'd have to get up. I did it for a while before telling him it wasn't for me. He just bought my share back and carried on.

I continued to go on training courses and sometimes Walter Winterbottom, the England manager, would attend Preston's games in London. One time we played at Tottenham, and he came back on our coach and sat next to me. He was always good to listen to, very knowledgable and a nice person who was a real gentleman.

I know some managers ruled with a bit of fear, like Stan Cullis at Wolves for example. Billy Wright once told me they used to **** themselves at half-time if it wasn't going well. They'd try and escape to have a pee and he'd lash into them. It was one style of management, and it was successful for Wolves.

Cliff Britton could sometimes get angry but he never swore

or anything like that. He'd get all worked up, and I hadn't seen that with Ted Fenton.

Though some players can respond to that, for others it's not the best way to deal with them. But sometimes it just builds up in a manager and he lashes out. Cliff wouldn't shout at Tom Finney - he might say a quiet word to him - and generally he didn't shout at anyone. Jimmy Milne would support Cliff and come around and have a quiet word. He was a very honest chap and North End through and through.

I didn't play much in the 1960-61 season, Tom Finney had already retired and generally the whole team was getting older. I wasn't playing regularly and I could see what was coming. I knew my days were numbered, but I'd had a good innings after coming into the game quite late.

The manager told me I wasn't being retained, and I believe another club, Lincoln City I think, were interested in me. But then Weymouth came in and offered me the position of player-manager.

Frank (right) entered into a brief partnership in a newsagent's shop in Preston with former Everton player Peter Corr.

Getting to work as player-manager of non-League Weymouth.

I can't remember the exact details, but somebody contacted the club to see if I'd contact them - I got in touch and I then went down for an interview and they offered me the job.

It meant another move, this time down to the south coast, and the funny thing was I'd been on £20 per week at Preston - the maximum wage at the time - and Weymouth upped that to £25 and I also got a car and a house. They were outside the Football League (in the Southern League) so the maximum wage didn't apply. It was crazy that I was dropping from the First Division to the Southern League, but getting more money! I never benefitted from the abolition of the maximum wage in 1961 which happened as I left Preston.

I wasn't exactly sure where Weymouth was, only that it was on the south coast somewhere.

I knew my time as a player was coming to an end, though I suppose I could have played in the lower divisions for a while, but that never really appealed to me. I'd been on coaching courses and I'd been at two clubs who talked about the game a lot, and I

Showing off his ball skills at Weymouth.

thought I'd like to try my hand at management. The previous manager at Weymouth had been Arthur Coles and he'd been there for some years. They always used to boast that they never finished below sixth in the table, but then again they had never won the title.

I think I am right in saying that someone at Stoke City knew I was being released by Preston and had told Weymouth.

I was impressed with the Weymouth set-up and their ground, which was called the Recreation Ground. It had a stand and covered terracing, and I read up a little about the club.

At the interview, their priority was having someone who could play and manage. They also wanted someone to recruit players, and I think they felt I had a lot of contacts I could use.

I'd had some injuries at Preston in 1960, including having a cartilage out and I was in Wrightington Hospital, near Wigan, watching the European Cup final of that year, when the great Real Madrid famously beat Eintracht Frankfurt 7-3 at Hampden Park in Glasgow. But I felt I was still OK to play.

I was nervous to start with as a manager, but I suppose that is normal. You're having to put your thoughts over and come up with new ideas and not everyone will agree with you.

Your first real test as a manager is when you put that first team sheet up. You can only pick 11 players and every player thinks they should be in the team, and someone usually challenges your selection. As the player-manager I also had to explain to the player I was replacing in a decent sort of way why I was picking myself and not him. It often led to confrontation and it was an eye-opener for me, but I suppose it prepared me to make some big decisions later in my career - like dropping Bobby Charlton!

I came from two good footballing clubs and I wanted the Weymouth fans to go home after games having watched some good football. I always tried to get the best out of the players and play football the right way - and not resort to kick and rush.

The first player I signed was a lad called Brian Bevan, who had played in the Football League for Bristol City, Carlisle and Millwall. He was a winger and I had been told he was available. He signed on a wall outside the Countess Wear Hotel in Exeter and I was really proud to have made my first signing.

He accepted the terms I offered, but it was a bit of a 'blind' signing as I had never seen him play. In those days, you often went on the number of games they had played in the Football League, and from a recommendation from someone you trusted. I assessed his character when I met him and I was quite happy having to make judgements like that.

Weymouth mostly trained on Tuesday and Thursday nights, and in pre-season we'd use the ground if conditions were all right. Quite often we'd train on the beach as well when the tide was out. The sand was good and the council were very helpful in leaving the illuminations on so we could train at night.

The players were obviously part-timers, and had other jobs like bricklaying or carpentry, and we had a friend of the club at Portland Naval base who found jobs for a lot of them. With the day job, and their money from playing for Weymouth, very often they were getting more than some Fourth Division players.

Sometimes they'd get a job in the summer looking after the deckchairs on the beach or something similar. Some of them had trades, John Hannigan (I think he came from Derby but he still lives in Portland) was an electrician and Des Jones, a Welsh lad who had League experience with Workington, was a bricklayer, so they often worked hard in the day before coming to training. It was my job to inspire them and not let them think they were knackered.

I'd train more often than the other players, but I would also go out looking at games and potential signings. At the end of the season I'd get in touch with the Players' Union and get a list of all the players who had been released by their clubs. I'd go away for a week, first to Manchester to the Players' Union offices to get the list, and then go round interviewing players to see if they would come down to Weymouth. I didn't hang around, I got the addresses off the Players' Union and used to go knocking on doors.

I tried to recruit Willie Carlin, who had been at Liverpool, but he said he wanted to stay in the League, though I did eventually sign him after I moved to Leicester City.

I got Tommy Spratt, a good inside-forward from Bradford Park Avenue, by knocking on his door and he was a big success at Weymouth. He subsequently joined me at Torquay and scored

18 goals from midfield in his first season when we won promotion to Division Three. Obviously there was a limited budget but you had licence to go beyond it if there was a player you really wanted. However there weren't mega-bucks available.

The Weymouth chairman was Reg Bartlett, a grocer in the town, but after a couple of years he was succeeded by Maurice Sapsworth - they were the two chairmen I worked for while I was there. I had a pretty good relationship with both of them. Reg tended to be a bit more cautious as he was a small shopkeeper and was worried about budgets and so on. I think Maurice ran a butcher's shop and he gave me a bit more money when he became chairman. He wanted to do well and we won the Southern League title during his chairmanship.

Sammy McGowan helped me at Weymouth. He had played for the club and was a nice Scots lad. He ran a pub with his wife Jenny not far from the ground and he was the team trainer. He had a lot of background knowledge of the club and about the players I had inherited and I gleaned plenty of information from him. We got on well, we'd do the training together and he had a likeable way. He'd have a joke with the players and they had a really good rapport with him.

I also had a good friend called Haydn Hill, who had played as an amateur goalkeeper for Sheffield Wednesday before the War. He was head of maths at Weymouth Grammar School for Boys and was in charge of the youth team I started.

We had a reserve team in the Western League and Haydn would keep me abreast of how the under-18 players were developing in the youth team.

I signed a goalkeeper, Kevin McLoughlin, who had played for Cardiff City when they were beaten 10-1 by Moscow Dynamo at Ninian Park just after the War. He was a schoolteacher who lived up near Salisbury and I signed him for the reserves. He never got into the first team but he was very reliable and he'd help with the team.

I was still playing as well and I couldn't be everywhere so to have these sort of people helping out with the reserves and youth team was invaluable. I trusted their judgement too.

I had learned a lot from my former managers, especially Cliff Britton, and like him I did get angry at times and bawl a player out. That sort of thing doesn't work for all players, but it does for some. Different players have different temperaments and it is a manager's job to use that to your advantage.

But I like to think I was always fair, especially when I was discussing terms with players, and I expected loyalty in return.

I liked to play football, but I also liked defenders to be safe and not take chances. I would get upset if we conceded bad goals. Tactics like 4-4-2 and 4-3-3 were just starting to come in, but generally it was still two wingers in a five-man forward line.

I only demanded from the players what I thought they were capable of. As long as they played to their maximum, that was good enough for me. Many of them had played at a higher level and dropped down so there was a pretty decent standard of football. A lot of League clubs had big staffs before the maximum wage was abolished, and they had to cut their staffs so it was a good time to recruit players for non-League football.

I had about 18 to 20 semi-professionals to choose from, and in the 1961-62 season, my first at the club, we finished sixth in the Southern League, despite making a slow start. We only won two of our first 13 league games, but an 8-1 home win over Cambridge City in late October saw us turn the corner.

We also reached the Third Round of the FA Cup after beating Dorchester Town, Barnet and Newport County. Newport were a League team then and I signed goalkeeper John Clarke from the Welsh club. I got him for just £50 and was rushing back to Weymouth with the good news when I got a speeding ticket - so in the end he cost the club a lot more than that!

We were one of three non-League clubs left in the FA Cup at the Third Round stage - Morecambe and King's Lynn were the others - and at that time they used to announce the draw on a Monday at 12.30pm on BBC Radio. It was a tradition that everyone would be around their radio at home or work listening to the draw, and we were all in the boardroom with baited breath.

All the directors were there hoping for an away tie at Manchester United or Arsenal, and a big payday. King's Lynn got Everton, which was a great draw, and then out came Morecambe versus Weymouth. Suddenly it was all doom and gloom - I think a couple of the directors almost fainted on hearing the news. It couldn't have been any worse could it? You battle all the way to that stage and then get another non-League team. After the euphoria of getting to the Third Round, it was a big let-down but we were determined to do things in style and we flew up to Blackpool from Bournemouth, stayed in a hotel on the seafront and went on a coach to Morecambe.

One of my old team-mates at Preston, Joe Dunn, was player-manager of Morecambe, having been released by North End at the same time as me. But he didn't play on the day because of a family bereavement.

I played and I think I got Man of the Match in a 1-0 win. Now we were dreaming of Manchester United or Arsenal again, and we were all around the radio again on the Monday lunchtime for the draw for the Fourth Round.

A lot of the big teams had already been drawn when out it came ... Preston North End versus Weymouth! The directors were disappointed it wasn't a bigger club but there was obviously a lot of interest in that I had only left Preston the season before. The national papers made a lot of it and once again we got the plane up to Blackpool and stayed at the same hotel on the sea front.

On the day of the game, there was a bit of fog around and the closer we got to Preston the thicker it became. At the ground it was really bad, but we got changed and the match kicked off. We played for 14 minutes and I maybe had two kicks of the ball and a throw-in, but I didn't know where I was most of the time. Our goalkeeper on the day was a chap called Billy Bly, who'd spent all of his career at Hull City. Cliff Britton had become manager of Hull after getting the sack when Preston had been relegated and I had asked him about a goalkeeper when Bob Charles had broken his finger in a previous game.

Cliff suggested Billy, even though he was 42. Cliff said Billy had played in his testimonial match a couple of months earlier and he'd done well. So he gave me Billy's phone number and I rang him and introduced myself and told him what I wanted and he sounded interested and said he would come down.

I arranged to meet him at King's Cross station and he signed at a tea shop at the station. The local press weren't totally impressed I was signing a 42-year-old goalkeeper but he was a fantastic person and he had dedicated his whole life to Hull City. He ran a newsagents up there as well, and was very unlucky to

Listening to the FA Cup draw on the radio (above) and preparing for a training session ahead of the Preston cup tie with (left to right) John Sheppard, Colin Court, Ron Fogg and Cliff Nugent.

Frank and some Weymouth players enjoying themselves at Blackpool in the build-up to the FA Cup tie at Preston, and having a team meal together at their Blackpool hotel.

have never won an international cap. He got a lot of injuries, breaking fingers and his wrist and all sorts, but he was a loyal one-club man.

Billy was a great professional, one of the most impressive players and one of the nicest people I ever met in the game. He was never any trouble, despite the fact he had to travel down from the north for most matches. He had a sister in Bournemouth and he used to stay with her at times, especially for midweek matches.

Anyway going back to the Preston game, the referee called the two captains together after about 14 minutes play and asked whether we wanted to carry on. It was decided we would have a break to see if the fog cleared up, so we went off the field and were in the dressing room when someone noticed Billy wasn't there.

I sent someone out to look for him - and he was still in goal! I asked him why he was still there and he said he thought we had Preston under pressure at the other end. In the end the game was abandoned, and replayed, on the following Monday night.

We spent the weekend in Blackpool and I had to phone up the bosses of some of the players saying they wouldn't be coming in to work on the Monday. Most of the Weymouth fans went back home, and then travelled up again on the day of the game. There were 18,000 at Deepdale on the Saturday, and then there were 27,000 for the rematch, so it proved a good payday for us. We lost 2-0 but gave a good account of ourselves against a top team and I was proud of our efforts.

Generally my time at Weymouth was successful, though things didn't always go to plan and there were times when I asked myself what would I do if they sacked me. I wasn't qualified to do anything else apart from going back to the railway. I didn't even have my own house at the time - it was a club house.

You are dealing with human beings, they all make mistakes, and for some reason sometimes you don't win matches you should have won. As player-manager I had to pick myself and in my early days at the club there was a player who played in my position and I was keeping him out of the team. He said he wasn't happy and wanted a transfer, so I said alright but that would have to wait as I didn't know what the team was like yet and I may need him in the future. I asked whether his wife would be happy for him to move and he said yes she would.

The next day there's a knock on my office door and it's his wife! And she said she wanted to stay in Weymouth. But she told me not to tell him, so as I've got his wife on my side, he's got no chance of moving. He did eventually leave, but only when I considered it to be in the best interests of the club.

On October 31, 1962, I had been scouting up at Bedford and was travelling back when I was involved in a car crash. It was around midnight with not much traffic around, and it was pitch black near Puddletown (north east of Dorchester). I was doing around 60mph and as I came around a corner there was a fellow in the middle of the road frantically waving a light to stop me. I slammed the brakes on, the car somersaulted and hit the bank before coming to a halt. I had blood all over me. Ann had bought me a seatbelt for my birthday - which was three weeks earlier and before seatbelts were compulsory - and I would probably have been killed had I not been wearing it.

There had been an accident further down on the next bend and the chap had seen my lights and was trying to get to the bend before me but didn't quite make it. The car was a write off and the police took me home. Luckily I was OK, but it was my third brush with death - after nearly drowning in that swimming pool back in Ireland and having the serious nose bleed at Preston - so the Good Lord certainly looked out for me.

A forerunner to Britain's Got Talent? Frank, one of the judges at Southern Television's 1960s talent show, Home Grown, congratulates heat winner Glenda Sambrook from Twyford in Hampshire. Glenda sang and played the piano.

I had a second cartilage operation on my left knee while I was at Weymouth and that finished my playing career. I played my last game in November 1963, and I remember it was the day after President Kennedy had been assassinated in America. Though the Weymouth board felt that having a player-manager was more cost-effective, they believed I was doing a good job and kept me on as manager.

My final season at Weymouth was 1964-65. We had finished sixth, third and seventh in the previous three seasons, and finally it all came good and we won the Southern League title. It was the first time the club had won the League and I felt we had been getting better and better during the time I was there. We had a civic reception and it was very special for the town.

We had a lot of quality in the side, and I always tried to add a bit more each season without changing things too much. I got players like Tommy Spratt, Bob Forrest, Colin Court, Alex

Weymouth in 1964-65. Back (left to right): Bob Forrest, Terry Gulliver, John Clarke, Phil Stocker, Jackie Hinchliffe, Tony Hobson. Front (left to right): John Hannigan, Tommy Spratt, Alex Jackson, Barry Hutchinson, Dave Camp.

SEASON TO REMEMBER 1964-65

WEYMOUTH CROWNED SOUTHERN LEAGUE CHAMPIONS

SOUTHERN LEAGUE

Aug 22	Cheltenham Town (a)	0-2		2,647
Aug 26	Nuneaton Borough (h)	4-0	Hutchinson 2, Hannigan, Camp	2,850
Aug 29	Cambridge United (h)	2-1	Hannigan, Hinchliffe	2,647
Sept 12	Folkestone Town (h)	5-1	Hutchinson 2, Camp, Hannigan, Spratt	2,366
Sept 14	Nuneaton Borough (a)	1-2	Hannigan	2,486
Sept 19	Margate (a)	2-0	Jackson, Spratt	2,432
Sept 21	Worcester City (a)	2-2	Hutchinson, Spratt	4,415
Sept 26	Bath City (h)	3-1	Spratt, Hannigan, Jackson	2,645
Sept 30	Chelmsford City (h)	3-2	Hutchinson, Hannigan, Camp	4,161
Oct 3	King's Lynn (a)	2-3	Hutchinson, Jackson	1,817
Oct 10	Bedford Town (a)	2-0	Hutchinson 2	2,067
Oct 24	Cambridge City (a)	2-0	Hutchinson, Spratt	2,456
Oct 31	Guildford City (h)	0-0		3,100
Nov 7	Wellington Town (a)	1-1	Hutchinson	1,614
Nov 21	Dartford (a)	1-0	Forrest	2,278
Nov 28	Wisbech Town (h)	7-3	Hutchinson 2, Hannigan 2, Forrest 2, Spratt	2,217
Dec 12	Cheltenham Town (h)	2-0	Hobson, Camp	2,300
Dec 19	Cambridge United (a)	2-2	Hannigan, Hutchinson	3,158
Dec 26	Yeovil Town (a)	1-0	Jackson	5,073
Jan 2	Worcester City (h)	3-1	Hutchinson 2, og	3,500
Jan 9	Hastings United (a)	1-2	Hutchinson	1,031
Jan 12	Bexley United (h)	4-0	Hutchinson, Spratt, Cribb, og	2,465
Jan 16	Folkestone Town (a)	4-3	Hutchinson 2, Camp, Spratt	1,188
Jan 23	Margate (h)	7-1	Spratt 5, Hutchinson 2	2,560
Jan 26	Rugby Town (a)	1-2	Hutchinson	1,084
Jan 30	Hastings United (h)	7-1	Hutchinson 3, Spratt 3, Camp	2,250
Feb 6	Bath City (a)	1-1	Jackson	2,038
Feb 13	King's Lynn (h)	4-0	Hinchliffe, Cribb, Jackson, Spratt	2,500
Feb 20	Bedford Town (h)	0-1		2,274
Feb 27	Chelmsford City (a)	2-3	Hutchinson 2	3,477
Mar 6	Cambridge City (h)	3-2	Cribb, Hutchinson, Spratt	3,200
Mar 13	Guildford City (a)	2-0	Hutchinson, Cribb	4,189
Mar 16	Yeovil Town (h)	3-0	Hutchinson 2, Hannigan	4,870
Mar 20	Wellington Town (h)	0-2		1,500
Mar 27	Bexley United (a)	2-1	Jackson, Cribb	930
Apr 7	Tonbridge (h)	0-0		2,500
Apr 12	Wisbech Town (a)	2-2	Hutchinson, Spratt	796
Apr 16	Romford (a)	0-2		3,500
Apr 17	Rugby Town (h)	6-1	Hutchinson 3, Hannigan, Spratt, Cribb	2,200
Apr 19	Romford (h)	1-2	Cribb	2,700
Apr 24	Tonbridge (a)	2-2	Spratt 2	1,583
Apr 29	Dartford (h)	2-1	Spratt 2	3,243

SOUTHERN LEAGUE CUP

Sept 2	Merthyr Tydfil (a)	0-1		3,986
Sept 9	Merthyr Tydfil (h)	2-0	Jackson 2	2,251
Oct 7	Gloucester City (h)	4-0	Hutchinson 2, Spratt 2	2,819
Nov 25	Hereford United (a)	2-2	Spratt, Hutchinson	4,095
Dec 16	Hereford United (h)	1-0	Jackson	2,615
Feb 17	Cheltenham Town (h)	2-1	Spratt, Camp	3,273
Mar 8	Hillingdon Borough (a)	6-1	Spratt 2, Hutchinson 2, Cribb 2	3.000
Apr 3	Cambridge United (h) F1	1-1	Spratt	4,093
Apr 10	Cambridge United (a) F2	0-2		4,200

FA CUP

Oct 17	Fareham Town (h)	3-2	Camp, Spratt, Hutchinson	3,738
Nov 14	Welton Rovers (a)	1-1	Hutchinson	2,500
Nov 18	Welton Rovers (h)	4-3	Hutchinson 2, Spratt, Hannigan	5,597
Dec 5	Bristol Rovers (a)	1-4	Spratt	12,469

Jackson, Billy Bly, John Hannigan and John Clarke to come down to Weymouth. We also had Barry Hutchinson, a big, strong centre-forward who led the line well and scored 36 goals in the League for us.

We were really strong at home in 1964-65 and scored lots of goals. We netted seven on three different occasions against Wisbech (7-3), Margate (7-1 when Tommy Spratt scored five) and Hastings (7-1 when both Spratt and Hutchinson netted hat-tricks) and six against Rugby Town (6-1). We had a real purple patch just after Christmas when we scored goals for fun, 28 of them in just seven games. We also reached the final of the Southern League Cup for the second successive season, but like the first time, we finished as losing finalists, this time beaten over two legs by Cambridge United.

During that last season, Dover wanted to talk to me but nothing came of it. I also went for interviews at two Football League clubs. I applied for the jobs at both Watford and Colchester, but Ken Furphy got the Watford job - I had a good interview but they felt that Ken had more League experience as he had managed at Workington - while at Colchester it went to Neil Franklin, who had returned from coaching in Cyprus. Benny Fenton, the brother of Ted, was manager at Colchester but he was going to Charlton and he said I had a good chance of getting it so I applied.

I don't know how true it is but I had a chat with Benny afterwards and he said that two of the directors didn't like Irishmen. Nowadays I could probably have charged them with the race relations act. How times change.

There were some good managers in non-League football then who went on to make a name for themselves in the League, the likes of my former team-mate Malcolm Allison (Bath City), Ron Saunders (Yeovil Town) and David Pleat (Nuneaton Borough). David told me once that when he took over at Nuneaton Borough, they wanted him to do for Nuneaton what Frank O'Farrell had done for Weymouth.

But my time at Weymouth was about to end and I was on my travels again. I never actually applied for the Torquay United job, and subsequently I never applied for any manager's job again.

All the clubs I later joined came in for me. As far as Torquay

Frank pictured at Plainmoor after taking over as manager of Torquay United, his first managerial post in the Football League.

were concerned, I had a call from the chairman Tony Boyce (he died a couple of years ago and I saw him the day before his passing in Newton Abbot Hospital where he had gone after a stroke). The call came completely out of the blue as I was preparing for another season with Weymouth. I had no idea whether they had sacked Eric Webber or not, but we agreed to meet in a hotel in Exeter and I had a meal with him and his wife Sheila.

Mr Boyce offered me an attractive package and he seemed like a decent bloke, and it was a chance for me to get into the Football League. My daughters, Bernadette and Catherine, were at a convent school at the time but Ann said you've got to take the opportunity - she was always like that - even though she had to change doctors and hospitals with her diabetes. So we folded up our tent and we moved on. I left Weymouth on pretty good terms, even though I think they were disappointed I was leaving. I had won the Southern League championship with the club and taken them to the Fourth Round of the FA Cup.

It was an opportunity I had to take, because you never knew if another one would come along. As it was quite a few did.

Anyway Torquay was my first port of call in the League and I kept the training staff they already had in place, in the shape of Jack Edwards and Harry Topping, who looked after the reserve team and also acted as physiotherapist. The Plainmoor ground wasn't as good then as it is today. It was open on the far side, and the Babbacombe End has since been developed, with the capacity much reduced. But it generated a great atmosphere and we got some good gates, sometimes up to 9,000. We also started experimenting by playing on Saturday evenings for a while and a lot of local footballers came along after their own games. That was one of Tony Boyce's ideas. He was a bright man and he was always looking for ways to increase the gates and get more money in. The club also had a very competent secretary in John Smith, and he had a very efficient secretary in Miss Newman.

The Saturday evening games were well supported but they did have an effect on the Football Pools. There was no lottery in those days and everybody did the Pools and they were based on afternoon games, so an evening kick-off kind of disrupted the system.

Talking tactics with trainer Jack Edwards (above) and Torquay United pictured in 1968-69 (below). Back (left to right): Ken Sandercock, John Benson, Andy Donnelly, Fred Binney, Bob Glozier. Middle (left to right): Jack Edwards (coach), Ronnie Barnes, John Bond, Robin Stubbs, Bill Kitchener, Ken Brown, John Rowlands, Micky Cave, Alan Smith, Don Mills (trainer). Front (left to right): Jimmy Dunne, Alan Welsh, Pat Morrissey, Frank O'Farrell (manager), Tony Scott, Bobby Baxter.

From the start as a manager, I didn't want my players getting booked for unnecessary things. I wanted them to play hard, but not stupidly. There's just no profit in that. If players made bad tackles through misjudgement, I was never hard on them, but if they were reckless and damage was caused, then I would be. To be honest I can't recall hardly any of my players being sent off during my managerial career, though famously George Best was dismissed at Chelsea for allegedly swearing at the referee!

One of the things people always ask me is how did I get the likes of John Bond, Ken Brown, Bill Kitchener and Tony Scott down from West Ham to play for Torquay. First of all they knew me and trusted me, and I also gave them a great deal that if they couldn't move down then I would allow them to train with West Ham during the week. Ron Greenwood was very helpful in letting them train there. They were only short-term signings and didn't want to move down to Devon, and I couldn't really insist on it. When you could attract players of their calibre, it made it a lot easier to convince other players to join Torquay as well.

We had about five club houses at the time, before the club eventually had to sell them. Often I would get a call from a neighbour of these houses saying the garden was overgrown, or weeds were growing into his garden, and I would send someone round to tidy up.

The one exception to that was John Smith, who was a West Ham schoolboy, then went to Tottenham, Coventry City and Leyton Orient before I signed him. He only came down because of Bondy and he hadn't been at Torquay long when I asked him how he was settling in at the house.

He said fine, he had got the garden dug and got the plants in. I had to laugh because I couldn't imagine a player doing that - and he really had. Sadly John was only 49 when he died in 1988.

Winning promotion to Division Three in my first season at Torquay was a great achievement, but it was achieved with quality players, many of whom had played at a higher level and who would be capable of performing well in a higher division.

It was tight at the top, and we finished third on 58 points, a point behind champions Doncaster Rovers and runners-up Darlington (at a time of two points for a win), and only two points ahead of Tranmere Rovers, who finished fifth and missed out on promotion. We led the table early on, despite losing 4-1 at Bradford City in our opening game, and were unbeaten at home until we suffered a hiccup in losing 4-1 to Stockport County in November. Darlington also won 4-0 at Plainmoor after Christmas, but we remained in the picture, although we lost three games out of four towards the end of the season to put ourselves under pressure.

We finished strongly, and were unbeaten in our last six games, a run that included a crucial 2-1 home win over Tranmere, and a promotion-clinching 0-0 draw at Darlington in our final game in front of a crowd of over 16,000.

Robin Stubbs was an outstanding centre-forward who had joined Torquay from Birmingham City and he scored 16 goals during the promotion campaign. He was strong, quick and good in the air and I think he could still have been playing at a higher level. He was single lad, something of a personality in the town and very popular with the ladies. He later married Anthea Redfern, who went on to take part in the BBC game show The Generation Game, and subsequently married her co-host, Bruce Forsyth.

We also had Tommy Spratt, who I brought with me from

One of the perks of playing for Torquay United? The Gulls players tackle a steep incline on the Devon coastal path during training.

SEASON TO REMEMBER 1965-66

TORQUAY UNITED PROMOTED TO DIVISION THREE (3RD PLACE)

DIVISION FOUR

Date	Opponent	Score	Scorers	Attendance
Aug 21	Bradford City (a)	1-4	Kirkman	3,472
Aug 25	Newport County (h)	1-0	Hellin	7,489
Aug 28	Chesterfield (h)	2-0	Clarke, Stubbs	5,509
Sept 4	Rochdale (a)	3-2	Spratt, Northcott, Kirkman	3,720
Sept 11	Luton Town (h)	2-0	Northcott	5,126
Sept 13	Newport County (a)	2-3	Rowland og, Spratt	3,827
Sept 18	Barrow (a)	0-2		4,714
Sept 22	Southport (h)	1-1	Wyatt	5,541
Sept 25	Hartlepool United (h)	2-0	Spratt, Stubbs	4,423
Oct 2	Doncaster Rovers (a)	1-0	Spratt (pen)	9,913
Oct 4	Bradford PA (a)	1-1	Benson	5,119
Oct 9	Port Vale (h)	1-0	Spratt	5,122
Oct 16	Halifax Town (a)	2-0	Spratt, Clarke	2,627
Oct 20	Barnsley (h)	3-0	Spratt 2 (1 pen), Wyatt	5,726
Oct 23	Chester City (h)	1-0	Clarke	6,470
Oct 30	Notts County (a)	1-1	King	7,174
Nov 6	Lincoln City (h)	4-1	Stubbs 3, Spratt	5,567
Nov 20	Stockport County (h)	1-4	King	5,040
Nov 23	Bradford PA (h)	2-1	Clarke, Stubbs	3,892
Nov 26	Tranmere Rovers (a)	1-0	Clarke	9,815
Dec 11	Barnsley (a)	0-1		4,646
Dec 27	Aldershot (h)	5-1	Spratt 2, Wyatt, Kearns og, Stubbs	8,257
Jan 1	Port Vale (a)	0-0		7,048
Jan 8	Darlington (h)	0-4		5,981
Jan 15	Chester City (a)	1-1	Smith	9,302
Jan 29	Bradford City (h)	4-3	Wolstenholme, Clarke, Wyatt, Spratt	5,779
Feb 5	Chesterfield (a)	1-1	Wyatt	4,808
Feb 12	Wrexham (h)	3-1	Clarke, Spratt, Barnes	4,654
Feb 16	Aldershot (a)	2-3	Spratt, Stubbs	2,865
Feb 19	Rochdale (h)	4-0	Stubbs 3, Clarke	5,504
Feb 26	Luton Town (a)	2-3	Stubbs, Barnes	9,271
Mar 3	Wrexham (a)	2-0	Stubbs, Spratt	10,141
Mar 12	Barrow (h)	0-1		5,513
Mar 19	Hartlepool (a)	2-0	Spratt, Stubbs	4,789
Mar 26	Doncaster Rovers (h)	0-0		8,645
Apr 2	Lincoln City (a)	1-1	Northcott	2,472
Apr 8	Crewe Alexandra (a)	1-2	Northcott	5,818
Apr 9	Colchester United (h)	0-1		7,844
Apr 11	Crewe Alexandra (h)	2-1	Stubbs 2	6,224
Apr 15	Stockport County (a)	0-1		4,278
Apr 23	Tranmere Rovers (h)	2-1	Northcott, Spratt	7,862
Apr 25	Southport (a)	3-3	Clarke, Northcott, Stubbs	3,960
Apr 30	Colchester United (a)	2-0	Clarke 2	5,932
May 2	Halifax Town (h)	1-0	Clarke	7,623
May 9	Notts County (h)	2-0	Benson, Spratt	8,928
May 21	Darlington (a)	0-0		16,469

FA CUP

Date	Opponent	Score	Scorers	Attendance
Nov 13	Shrewsbury Town (a)	1-2	Smith	6,896

LEAGUE CUP

Date	Opponent	Score	Scorers	Attendance
Sept 1	Shrewsbury Town (a)	0-3		4,820

Weymouth, Dougie Clarke, who had experience at Bury and Hull City and Ronnie Barnes, who had played for Blackpool, Norwich City and Peterborough.

John Benson was the captain, and he possessed fantastic energy and commitment. He never gave up and was a terrific competitor. Later on during my time at Torquay, Fred Binney came through the ranks - he later became a prolific goalscorer with a number of clubs - and I also signed Jim Fryatt, another striker who scored plenty of goals in the lower divisions.

John Bond was the first of a handful of players I signed from West Ham, and I insisted that when we played at home the players living and training in London had to be in Torquay the day or evening before the game for my peace of mind. I didn't want to be worrying about players getting delayed and missing the game if they travelled on the day of the match.

There was one occasion when, for his own reasons, John decided to travel down on the Saturday of a game. I only found out when I phoned his lodgings on Saturday morning. I wanted to talk to him about some matter. His landlord said he was not there and he was travelling down by car that morning. We were playing Bury in a Division Three top of the table clash and the match was billed as the prime game on Match of the Day that night.

I had to take John's name off the team sheet and put in a replacement from the reserve team, who were travelling to play an away game somewhere. I could not risk the possibility of fielding ten men in a big match that was being screened on Match of the Day. When John arrived at Plainmoor, he went to the dressing rooms and saw his name had been removed from the team sheet. He knocked at my office door wanting to know why we wasn't playing.

He did not want to accept my reason and being angry, he went away and wrote a not very polite letter. I had promised him he would be back in the team the following week - he was just not going to play against Bury. I think his greatest worry was facing the West Ham players at training on the Monday morning and explaining why he hadn't been on television. Anyway we won the game 3-0 so I felt my decision had been the correct one.

Some years later when we met, both us of having gone to

different clubs and not seeing each other for a while, we recalled the incident. I did remind him how I kept my promise and played him the following week. I had forgotten some of the detail and he had to remind me that I picked him to play outside-left! (he was a full-back). We had a laugh about it, and I told him I never said where I would play him, just that he would be playing.

We are the best of friends now and John found out himself when he went into management that you have to make those kind of difficult decisions, and risk falling out with people as a result. You can't be one of the boys anymore and you have to grow away from them a little as you often have to make decisions that will hurt players.

John could consider himself lucky that I didn't order him in for extra heading practise - he never did like heading the ball!

Towards the end of the promotion season, another important player in the team had caused me a headache over a breach of club discipline. Back then there were no motorways like there are today, and when we were playing away at places like Hartlepool or Darlington, we used to leave on a Friday morning and travel north, meandering along the old A5 and A6 roads. On our return after the match we would sometimes stop over in Leeds on the

Frank goes back to his roots to shovel some coal on the Devon-based Dartmouth steam train alongside driver Bob Hill.

Saturday night, and resume our journey after breakfast on Sunday morning, arriving back in Torquay around tea-time on Sunday evening - talk about a safari.

One Saturday night when we stayed in Leeds, I got up to go to early Mass on Sunday morning. Dougie Clarke, who was also a Catholic, walked with me to the church, which was not far from the hotel.

On our way down the stairs of the hotel, we heard footsteps in front of us. I thought someone else must be going to early Mass. When we got outside we looked to see who had also got up so early and who should it be but one of my players walking arm in arm with a lady! He didn't see us and when we got back to the hotel, and had finished breakfast, I called all the players together and said "Will the player (who I did not name) who I saw leaving the hotel earlier with a woman come to my office on Monday morning." I heard later there was a joke going around the dressing room that there was a queue outside Frank's office on the Monday morning!

In deciding what punishment to mete out to the player, I had to balance out the obvious need to punish him and at the same time not upset him too much to cause a loss of form and endanger our chances of promotion as he was a key player. I decided to give him a good lecture about his breach of discipline - and told him I would have to ponder what the most appropriate punishment would be but for now I would delay my decision.

He continued to play in the final few matches, and we gained promotion to Division Three. At the end of the season I called him into my office and told him I was fining him. He was not at all pleased, and though he continued to play for the club for a while, he then asked for a transfer and I let him go. We have met on a number of occasions since and we always share a laugh about the incident.

We did well in our first season in Division Three and finished seventh, just four points behind second-placed Middlesbrough, who were promoted. Since the maximum wage had been abolished, it meant that clubs were letting some quality players leave and I tried to work that to Torquay's advantage.

On the other side of the coin, it was never easy telling a young player you didn't think he was good enough and were releasing him. I had to do it at all my clubs and it never got any easier. I always told them I'd do whatever I could to help and I hope I was always as kind and considerate as I possibly could have been.

Sometimes the parents of the younger players were more difficult, challenging you and saying they didn't agree with you. I always replied that if I'd made the wrong decision and your son makes it elsewhere I'd be delighted for you, but I have to make this decision now. Nobody would be happier than me if he went somewhere else and made it.

In the 1967-68 season, my third at Torquay, we were very close to winning promotion to Division Two. I was gradually building what I felt was a very decent team and during the summer I had brought in Bobby Baxter and Jimmy Dunne, an Irish lad from Fulham, while Ken Brown, Tony Scott and Bill Kitchener all arrived from West Ham, though Bill was only on loan to start with.

Bill had an excellent left-foot and could play at either left-back or centre-half. He was very solid and joined the police force after hanging up his boots.

We were unbeaten in our first ten matches and led the table in October. The 3-0 win over Bury in the Match of the Day game took us clear at the top in mid-March, but then we fell away disappointingly, and only won three of our last 12 matches. We

lost both our last two matches at Scunthorpe United (0-2) and Reading (0-4) and it meant we finished fourth, three points behind Bury, who were second and promoted alongside Oxford United.

One person who was an important part of the Torquay club for many years was Ben Street. His wife,

Frank completes the signing of Bill Kitchener, one of a handful of West Ham players he recruited at Torquay United.

Evelyn, used to say he was married to the club because he spent more time at Plainmoor than he did at home. Ben was a former merchant seaman and a jack of all trades. He had keys for everywhere at the club - he would open up in the morning and then close up at night. He did all sorts of jobs, including serving at the bar in the boardroom on matchdays. Evelyn used to serve teas in the guest room on matchdays along with another lady, Gladys. All small clubs can identify with people like Ben, Evelyn and Gladys. The club would just not have functioned properly without them.

As for my own position, after turning down approaches from Carlisle United, Bolton Wanderers and Ipswich Town, I always said to Tony Boyce that if a job came along that I thought was right for me, I'd go for it because I didn't want people to get the impression I wasn't ambitious. I knew I wasn't going to stay at Torquay for the rest of my career, and Tony knew it too.

One of the jobs I was offered while at Torquay was that of Ipswich Town manager. I travelled up there to meet John Cobbold, the chairman, and he couldn't have been nicer. I deliberated for a while before deciding not to take it, but it was a very hard decision, having dealt with the nicest people you could wish to meet. It was my decision and I never ever dwelt on what might have been had I taken the post. Bobby Robson was appointed as Ipswich manager and he went on to have a great career as a manager, eventually managing England as well.

Some time after that I got an invitation from Alf Pallett, the Leicester City chairman, to meet him in the Charing Cross Hotel in London. He offered me the manager's post and after discussing things with Tony Boyce, who wanted me to stay at Torquay, I decided to accept the offer.

Leicester were in a difficult situation, struggling at the bottom of the First Division table having won only three of their opening 21 games, but when you take over at a new club that is often the case. Usually managerial jobs only come about when teams are going through a bad time - it is rare a manager gets sacked when he's top of the table! But that's the challenge, you have to go in and improve things as quickly as possible.

EVENTS OF 1968

The Kray twins were arrested and jailed for gangland killings.

Martin Luther King was assassinated in the USA.

The last passenger steam train ran in the UK from Liverpool to Carlisle.

Christian Barnard performed the first successful heart transplant.

Manchester United won the European Cup,
beating Benfica 4-1 in extra-time at Wembley.

Frank O'Farrell was appointed manager of Leicester City.

4

JOY AND PAIN

Que sera, sera,
Whatever will be will be,
We're going to Wem-ber-lee,
Que sera, sera.

Doris Day (Livingston & Evans)

I LIKED the idea of working in the Midlands as you were within travelling distance of a lot of football. It was a big football area with Nottingham, Derby and Birmingham close to Leicester, and I wasn't isolated like at Weymouth and Torquay. Allan Brown, the Luton Town manager, was also in for the Leicester job and he was subsequently sacked by Luton for applying for it. Ironically he was then snapped up by Torquay to succeed me as manager at Plainmoor.

Leicester were a well-established club, had a good reputation and had a lot of local lads in the team. I took Malcolm Musgrove to Filbert Street with me. He had recently left Aston Villa, where he had been coach and had developed a good youth policy. I knew him well, he was a person I could trust and I knew we could work together. I needed someone like that as I was jumping from the Third Division to the First Division, and there would be more to do, more calls on my time, so I would have to delegate to someone I trusted. I trusted Malcolm, which is why I took him to both Leicester and later to Manchester United. He knew my ideas and would carry them out on the training field.

Matt Gillies, who had been manager at Leicester before me, was very helpful and showed me around. He had been offered the Nottingham Forest job but had been at Leicester for ten years and had a nice feeling for the club. I stayed on good friendly terms with him after that and it was he who in due course told me that

95

An early session at Leicester's training ground at Belvoir Drive alongside Andy Lochhead (left) and Malcolm Musgrove.

Matt Busby and Manchester United wanted to talk me.

One of the first things I found out early at Leicester was when I went down to the boot room and saw the state of the training boots. The players were leaving after training and just chucking their boots in, not even cleaning them or anything. I think that's the first thing I did, I said to the players that the training boots are an absolute disgrace. They are your tools so you take care of them. When you've finished with them, clean them, or you can come back in the afternoon and clean them then.

It was an attitude of mind that I had to change. Players must not be sloppy as that can carry into games. It was a wake-up call for some that things had to be done better.

The name most people will remember from Leicester at that time is Peter Shilton, but we had a lot of decent players like Peter Rodrigues, a Welsh international full-back, David Nish, the captain, and Allan Clarke up front. Andy Lochhead, a big Scot, was at centre-forward and there were a number of local players who had come through the ranks along with Shilton and Nish - the likes of Graham Cross, Rodney Fern and Paul Matthews.

Leicester had a good youth policy and the local players were generally quiet lads - they didn't have the swagger of the Cockneys or Liverpool boys. They were a nice bunch, very unassuming, but perhaps lacking a bit of aggression. Later on I signed Bobby Kellard from Bristol City and Willie Carlin, a Liverpudlian from Notts County who I had tried to sign at Weymouth, and they got stuck in and gave us some extra bite. They were like two little street fighters - but they had quality as well.

Ann and I lived in a hotel when I first joined Leicester, before finding a nice house on the Loughborough Road, and the girls enrolled at Loughborough Convent.

Obviously the job was a lot more high profile than at Torquay and the national newspapers wanted to interview me all the time.

Brian Clough and Peter Taylor were just up the road at Derby County, and I knew them from their Fourth Division days at Hartlepools. Peter rang me once at Torquay and said he was fed up at Hartlepools and could I find him a job somewhere. I told him I would recommend him if I heard of anything. Eventually Clough and Taylor moved together to Derby and then to Nottingham Forest. I always felt the relationship was a little fractious and they did eventually fall out - but they had great success together.

Frank shares a joke with the Leicester City squad. Pictured (left to right) are Andy Lochhead, John Sjoberg, Allan Clarke, Mike Stringfellow, Peter Rodrigues, Bobby Roberts, Malcolm Manley, David Nish, Graham Cross, Frank, Malcolm Musgrove and at the front are Bobby Mackay and Peter Shilton.

I found Bill Shankly a particularly interesting character, especially when we drew Liverpool in the FA Cup in my first season. The game at Filbert Street was postponed six times, and every time Bill came down on his own to be at the pitch inspection. He didn't need to be there, and I don't know whether he was suspicious of what was going on, but I was surprised he kept travelling all that way.

The pitch at Leicester was bad and the groundsman Doug had a thankless task. As a team the pitch did us few favours. We experimented with a big balloon with warm air in at one stage, but the wind and sun couldn't get in so it didn't last.

Shankly had played for Preston before me and I know he adored Tom Finney. Everyone knows about Shankly's witticisms and sayings and I took him to lunch when he came down for those pitch inspections and I found him really fascinating. He had a soft nature, and he'd talk about people he knew and his family, revealing things I didn't expect. I was impressed with the way he talked and his love for his family. From a distance I didn't think he'd be that kind of person. Later when I went to Manchester United, he rang and told me that I had a difficult job on my hands.

The Liverpool cup tie was in the Fifth Round after we had beaten Barnsley and Millwall. Ironically I had been knocked out of the FA Cup earlier in the season at Torquay, and I joked that it was a good job managers couldn't be cup-tied.

We beat Barnsley in a replay and then won 1-0 at Millwall with a goal from Lenny Glover. Leicester had a bit of a reputation at the time for being a good cup team after losing in the FA Cup finals of 1961 and 1963, and though our main priority was to avoid relegation, the cup wins could only be a boost to us to give the players confidence in the battle to avoid going down.

Leicester's record against Liverpool had been quite good in previous seasons and I am sure they would have preferred to have met someone else. When the tie finally went ahead, we drew 0-0 so had to go to Anfield for a replay.

That proved a wonderful night for us, with Peter Shilton saving a penalty from Tommy Smith following a handball from John Sjoberg, and Shanks having to take Roger Hunt off. I don't think Roger was too happy to be substituted. I had got Shilton practising saving penalties and that paid off. We won 1-0 with a headed goal by Andy Lochhead, from a Len Glover cross, and we were in the last eight. I was delighted with the result, though I may not have shown it like some of the managers do today, prancing about on the touchline. We also felt that if we could win at Liverpool, we could beat anyone and it raised our hopes that we could stave off relegation.

The Sixth Round took us to Mansfield Town, which was a good draw, though it could also have been a banana-skin. We won 1-0 again on a bog of a pitch with a goal from Rodney Fern, and were into the semi-finals.

At the same time we were still having a lot of matches postponed, especially at Filbert Street. I was on the phone an awful lot trying to rearrange League games, and I had to call Bill Nicholson three times to postpone the Tottenham fixture, but he was very understanding. Most of the other managers were too.

The semi-final was against West Bromwich Albion, who had won the FA Cup the previous year. Alan Ashman was their manager, and he was a thoroughly decent chap. The game was at Hillsborough, which in those days held 60,000. It had that big Spion Kop and was a fine ground. I had some nerves before the game but I made sure I didn't convey them to the team.

We won 1-0 again, this time with a late goal from Allan Clarke. It was a marvellous day for the club, the fans and the city of Leicester, though in the background there was our struggle to stay in Division One. Clarke was a great goalscorer, though he wasn't particularly outgoing. He tended to be a bit reserved and kept himself to himself.

There was plenty of banter in the dressing room by now, with Lenny Glover, a Londoner, always quite bright, and Bobby Roberts, a Scot, always full of confidence. Shilton was very focused and extremely ambitious. He would always want to do extra training and he'd ask me to give him a couple of apprentices to cross balls for him. He knew he could coach himself and he'd have them crossing balls from different angles for hours.

Leicester had sold Gordon Banks to Stoke City because they had Shilton pushing for a place in the first team when he was 16 or 17. He was good enough to be in the team at that age. He had supreme confidence, and I understand that part of his growing up included hanging off the banisters at home to strengthen and stretch his arms and legs. He was one of the most committed players I ever met. Even if he'd had a couple of differences with you - and we did have one or two fall-outs - he wouldn't take it onto the field.

If he blamed himself for three goals in a season he'd had a bad year - he was that much of a perfectionist and set such high standards. He was a brilliant goalkeeper and the ultimate professional.

I liked Peter and there was never any animosity between us. I met him years later when he was at Plymouth Argyle. My grandson Richard was playing in goal for his school team and I went to watch. They'd put him in goal because he was the tallest player in school, and he let in two goals. One was an own goal and the other a defender made a bad pass, but he was upset after the game. I said it wasn't his fault, so don't worry. Anyway I took him down to Plymouth to watch Peter doing some training. I gave Peter a nod and a wink and said this is my grandson and he's a goalkeeper so can you teach him a few things. He gave the lad a bit of coaching and some good advice.

So to the final against Manchester City at Wembley. I had been to Wembley to watch the 1966 World Cup final - I drove up from Torquay on the day with Tony Cavanagh, a club director - and I was also there for the 1948 Olympic games, when Fanny

LEICESTER CITY IN THE 1968-69 FA CUP

Jan 4	3rd Round	Barnsley (a)	1-1	Glover	25,099
Jan 8	Replay	Barnsley (h)	2-1	Fern, Glover	31,814
Jan 25	4th Round	Millwall (a)	1-0	Glover	31,480
Mar 1	5th Round	Liverpool (h)	0-0		42,002
Mar 3	Replay	Liverpool (a)	1-0	Lochhead	54,666
Mar 8	6th Round	Mansfield Town (a)	1-0	Fern	23,500
Mar 29	Semi-final	West Brom (Hillsborough)	1-0	Clarke	53,207

1969 FA CUP FINAL - Wembley Stadium, April 26
MANCHESTER CITY 1 (Young 24) LEICESTER CITY 0
Manchester City: Harry Dowd, Tony Book, Glyn Pardoe, Mike Doyle, Tommy Booth, Alan Oakes, Mike Summerbee, Colin Bell, Francis Lee, Neil Young, Tony Coleman.
Leicester City: Peter Shilton, Peter Rodrigues, David Nish, Bobby Roberts, Alan Woollett, Graham Cross, Rodney Fern, David Gibson, Andy Lochhead, Allan Clarke, Len Glover (Malcolm Manley).
Referee: George McCabe (Sheffield).

Blankers-Koen, the famous Dutch athlete, won four gold medals.

We stayed in Surrey at the same hotel England used, and on the Friday went to inspect the Wembley pitch. It wasn't in the best of condition as they'd had the army bands playing on it during the week.

During the match, I was interviewed on the touchline by Peter Lorenzo. The BBC had asked if I was happy to do it and stuck a microphone in front of me a couple of times for an update on how the match was going. To be honest I found it a distraction and I felt like I might miss something on the pitch. But it was a new innovation, I knew Peter quite well from the time he was a sports reporter on the Stratford Express and I did it to help him. They didn't continue with it though.

Joe Mercer and Malcolm Allison were in charge of Manchester City, and it's fair to say that Malcolm and me were quite different characters and though friends, we were never bosom pals. We had played together at West Ham, and I had met him again when he was at Bath City, and I was at Weymouth. He was always very flamboyant and had built up a great reputation as a coach.

There was a discussion in the build-up to the game about what kit we would wear, as both teams wore blue. In the end they played in red and black stripes and we used our normal blue and white kit.

There is no doubt we went into the game as underdogs and with injury problems but considering our run, we were quite confident, despite still struggling near the bottom of the Division One table. Forty or more years on, I remember a lot of the game passed me by, but I can still recall that the noise was almost deafening.

We certainly had our chances. Allan Clarke, who was made Man of the Match, knocked one header down for Andy Lochhead and had it been the other way round - Andy heading down to Allan - then we probably would have scored. Peter Rodrigues also had a very good chance early on and we should have taken the lead.

In the end it took a great shot from Neil Young to beat Peter Shilton. We allowed Mike Summerbee to get to the byline too easily, and he cut the ball back for Young. We got caught out, and

Clockwise from top left: Frank celebrates after Leicester had beaten West Bromwich Albion 1-0 in the FA Cup semi-final at Hillsborough; proudly leading Leicester out at Wembley alongside Manchester City's Joe Mercer; presenting the 1969 FA Cup final Man of the Match award to Leicester's Allan Clarke and the goal from Manchester City's Neil Young (not in picture) flashes past Peter Shilton, and Alan Woollett and Peter Rodrigues on the line.

they profited from it, but football is often about ifs and buts.

I think we gave a good account of ourselves. We had the disappointment of having lost, but we thought we'd played well, and felt we could save ourselves from relegation if we could carry that kind of performance into our remaining League games.

We had five Division One matches left and we needed seven points. We only got five. We beat Sunderland 2-1, when Alistair Brown scored twice on his debut, and Spurs 1-0, drew 1-1 at Everton but lost 2-1 at Ipswich Town, and then 3-2 in our final game at Manchester United.

We needed to win at Old Trafford but it was obviously a hard place to go and get a result. It was either Coventry or us who were going to go down along with Queens Park Rangers. The fact that Coventry stayed up had a lot to do with our game at Highfield Road towards the end of the season. We got a penalty decision in our favour only for the referee to go over to a linesman and change his mind! Coventry then went on to score a late winner.

Frank shakes hands with Matt Busby after the 3-2 defeat at Old Trafford sent Leicester down to Division Two.

Coventry manager Noel Cantwell, a mate of mine at West Ham and a former Manchester United player, was in the stands at our final game at Old Trafford and Pat Crerand later recalled in his autobiography that Noel had offered the United players a cash incentive to win the game. It's a good job nobody found out about that at the time.

It was Matt Busby's last game in charge and United didn't really have anything to play for, and although we took an early lead, they hit back to win 3-2 with goals from George Best, Denis Law and Willie Morgan. At the end of the match, Matt said "Hard luck Frank - the strength of a man is how he recovers from adversity." That bucked me up to face the players and start the rebuilding job.

All the same, it was a time of very mixed emotions. We'd reached the FA Cup final and played well at Wembley, and now here we were relegated to Division Two. A double whammy one could say. This was also the time when Leicester were appointing a new chairman, with Alf Pallett being replaced by Len Shipman. I was sorry to see Alf go, but Len was clearly an ambitious man - his family were hauliers and coal merchants in Leicester - and his son Terry was also on the board. They spent a bit of money when we got relegated - we had got £160,000 selling Allan Clarke to Leeds United - so we had the funds.

Neither Shilton nor Clarke wanted to play in Division Two after we were relegated. Clarke complained he'd come from a struggling club at Fulham and now he was at another struggling club and wasn't happy. I could understand as he was a top-class player, but he also moaned I was making him defend too much. I never expected him to be defending all the time but when you lose the ball, everybody needs to defend then. But they were just excuses, he wasn't happy and he wasn't the most cheerful character either.

Shilton was different. He was a local lad and had a lot of feeling for the club. He had signed a contract but he wanted to play for a bigger club because he was ambitious and felt he couldn't achieve what he wanted to achieve at Leicester, especially in the Second Division. I told him if you're the best goalkeeper in the country, even in the Second Division, you'll be selected for England and I think he got his first cap while at Leicester. But he wasn't happy and wanted to move to a bigger club. Strangely enough when he did eventually move, it was to Stoke City, and not to a club like Manchester United, Liverpool or Arsenal.

Neither of them put it in writing as the evidence would be there and they wouldn't get the percentage of their transfer fee. Peter knuckled down and eventually he went after I left the club.

But Clarke asked me four times for a move - he made it plain that he didn't want to play in the Second Division. Unlike Shilton, Clarke was more detached. Leicester didn't mean anything to him and eventually we sold him.

We beat Birmingham City 3-1 on the opening day of the 1969-70 season, won five of our first seven games and were always there or thereabouts near the top of the table.

I bought John Farrington, a winger, from Wolves a couple of months into the season, and he fitted in well, and contributed some important goals. We were unbeaten in November, with Rodney Fern scoring a memorable hat-trick in a 3-2 win at Bolton, but then had a bad December, losing 2-1 at home to Cardiff City, 1-0 at Sheffield United and 3-0 at Norwich City, and drawing 2-2 at home to Hull City. We also lost both League games in January, 2-0 at home to Swindon and 2-1 at Watford.

But we picked up again in the final run-in, winning 1-0 at Birmingham with a goal from Farrington, drawing 1-1 at promotion rivals Huddersfield Town and beating Preston North End 3-0, Blackburn Rovers 2-1 and Sheffield United 2-1 at home.

But the heavy Filbert Street pitch was always a handicap and in the end, a 0-0 draw at home to Blackpool in a mudbath over Easter, when we should have won, proved decisive. We had gone into the game on the back of four successive wins, including a 1-0 triumph at Oxford United on the Good Friday and a comprehensive 5-0 romp at Charlton Athletic on the Saturday.

We only lost one of our last 13 games - a 4-1 defeat at Hull City - but that lost point on Easter Tuesday in front of a crowd of over 32,000 ultimately proved vital and Blackpool and Huddersfield went up and we finished third, two points behind Blackpool.

Ironically we lost in the FA Cup to Liverpool. We were focused on getting promotion, but beat First Division sides Sunderland (1-0) and Southampton (4-2 in a replay at Filbert Street) to reach the last 16 before losing 2-0 to Liverpool in a replay at Filbert Street on a pitch that resembled a beach.

The players, the staff and myself were all bitterly disappointed that we had failed to win promotion back to Division One at the first attempt, and we talked and worked long hours in the summer analysing what went wrong and how we could go one better the following season.

During the summer of 1970 I went to the World Cup in Mexico. Leicester paid my fare and I went with a group of managers, including Bobby Robson, Alan Ashman, Dave Sexton and Bertie Mee. We saw England versus Brazil, when Gordon Banks made that fantastic save from Pele, and the West Germany match in the quarter-final when England surrendered a 2-0 lead to lose 3-2 in extra time. We were also at the final when Brazil beat Italy 4-1, and that was quite an experience. We even found an English pub over there that did bangers and mash and a pint.

It was great watching the Brazilians, and their training sessions always had a big following. We also took the opportunity to visit the International Shrine of Our Lady of Guadeloupe and that was very impressive.

About this time, I was approached by a TV producer called Paul Ellis, who said he wanted to do an educational 'Can You Manage' series for BBC 2 on different areas of industry. He wanted to do football as well, and wanted to use either me or Alec Stock, who was manager of Fulham.

I can't remember if I got paid or not, but I thought it was good promotion for the club, as well as for me, and I quite enjoyed it. They came into the dressing room for team talks, filmed the signing of players and also came to games. It turned out to be

Matt Busby tips Frank for a big future in the national press.

TIPS FOR THE TOP

Frank has that way with him!

THE TOP managers of the Sixties have been looking at the men they believe will be making an impact in the game as managers of the Seventies.

Sir Matt Busby, of Manchester United, is convinced that Leicester's Frank O'Farrell is booked for greatness.

"He has a way with him—a presence if you like," says Sir Matt. "He has a personality that strikes you: a quality that convinces you he knows what he is doing.

" I particularly like the way he handles difficult situations. The way he got Peter Shilton to re-sign is a good example. And I think he has a good knowledge of the game."

SIR MATT BUSBY . . . "O'Farrell aims to get there."

FRANK O'FARRELL . . . knocking on door of Division One.

quite a popular series, but I didn't change the way I conducted myself for the cameras. I just acted normal.

I am what I am and throughout my career, I have never tried to be something I wasn't. I'd never deliberately fall out with anybody but sometimes in football you'd upset people as their expectations or ideas wouldn't always match yours. I'd be miserable if we lost games, but I was never one to start throwing crockery around.

We had quite a good team spirit going at Leicester the following season, which ended up with us winning promotion back to Division One. Len Glover used to travel up from London but I made him stay in Leicester after the home matches. He didn't like it but I told him we were all in this together. If we lost at home and we all got stick in the local paper, it wasn't fair Len was down in London avoiding it. Eventually he bought a house in Leicester and is still living there today. When he first came to live in Leicester he was quite the squire of the county. He couldn't see any place as nice as Peckham but he settled down well and was a key player.

David Nish was a clever and articulate grammar school lad who captained by example, and who was also a terrific penalty taker, and we had two honest and tough centre-halves in Graham Cross and John Sjoberg. But every player knew he had 10 friends

Frank receives one of his four Manager of the Month awards - for November 1970 at Leicester City.

working for him in every game. If he was slightly below his best, the others would make up for it. Then the next week he would be helping someone else out.

I also added Bobby Kellard and Willie Carlin to the squad. We had a really good chief scout, Ray Shaw, who'd been a trainer at Aston Villa and Birmingham City and he recommended both. He was a loyal man, and a very good judge of a player. I actually went and watched Kellard myself as he cost £50,000, the biggest fee we paid out at the time.

We lost 1-0 at home to Cardiff City in our opening game, but we soon bounced back with a 3-1 victory on the road at Queens Park Rangers. We then played with a lot of confidence and after a 2-2 home draw with Carlisle United, we beat Bristol City 4-0, with future England full-back Steve Whitworth making his debut in the game.

I felt before the season started that we had young players who would improve, and that was certainly the case. Whitworth came in and did very well, as did Alistair Brown, who was the team's top scorer. He didn't have a lot to say for himself off the field, but on it he had a good stature and physique and he scored some important goals. Rodney Fern also came back into the team and did an excellent job. He had great natural ability.

FOOTBALL MANAGERS AWARD
ENGLAND

This is to Certify that

Frank O'Farrell

Manager of

Leicester City Football Club

has been nominated by a
panel of Leading British Sportswriters as
THE FOOTBALL MANAGER OF THE MONTH

November 1970

This certificate is awarded to the Football Manager whose club is a member of The
Football League or The Scottish Football League and who, in the opinion of the
judges, has personally given most to his club to help them fulfil their ambitions.

MANAGING DIRECTOR
ARTHUR BELL & SONS LTD.
SCOTCH WHISKY DISTILLERS.
PERTH SCOTLAND

I won one of my four Manager of the Month awards in November 1970 when we won three and drew one of our four League games. That meant four gallon bottles of Bell's whisky, but I don't drink it so three of them are still down in my cellar. The other one I gave to an old people's home.

We encountered a couple of hiccups, like losing 3-0 at Hull City in December and then suffering a surprise 4-1 home defeat to

Birmingham City just after Christmas, but they were few and far between. In fact after that defeat by Birmingham - on January 16 - we didn't lose another League game, stringing together a run of 17 unbeaten matches.

We finally won promotion by winning 1-0 at Bristol City in our penultimate game, and clinched the title with a 2-1 win at Portsmouth on the final Saturday of the season. The win at Fratton Park also messed up the Portsmouth players getting a big bonus. They were going to get £500 if they hit 35 points and all they needed was a draw. We were very strong defensively and only conceded two goals in our last nine away matches, and one of them came in the 89th minute at Portsmouth. There was a pitch invasion after the game by the travelling Leicester fans, the first I can ever remember.

We were presented with the Second Division trophy at John Sjoberg's testimonial match at Filbert Street, which attracted a crowd of 22,825 and earned John £8,300 for 13 years' loyal service to the club. I was saddened to learn that John had died in 2008.

We also had another good run in the FA Cup, beating Notts County, my old club Torquay United and Oxford United to reach the Sixth Round. We went out 1-0 to Arsenal in a controversial replay at Highbury when we had a perfectly good goal from Rodney Fern disallowed. The referee, Jim Finney, said Fern had his hand on the shoulder of a defender. But nobody liked meeting Leicester in the FA Cup in those days.

I felt I got a fair crack from the press during my managerial career, and especially at Leicester. The press had their jobs to do, and I don't think I ever fell out with any of them. Sometimes they wrote stuff I thought was harsh, and some papers were worse than others. I developed a good relationship with a Scot called Jimmy Martin on the Leicester Mercury. He was a really nice chap. Of course the papers were a lot different to today's - and there are virtually no Saturday night sports papers now. Most major towns had them then, on green, pink or buff paper.

I also got on well with Roland Orton, who ran a local news agency in Leicester, and of course local radio was just starting, and that gave me the opportunity to get over to the fans what I was trying to do at the club. Barrie Eccleston was one of the journalists at BBC Leicester who I used to chat to regularly.

SEASON TO REMEMBER 1970-71

LEICESTER CITY CROWNED DIVISION TWO CHAMPIONS

DIVISION TWO

Aug 15	Cardiff City (h)	0-1		27,578
Aug 22	QPR (a)	3-1	Brown, Kellard, Farrington	17,090
Aug 29	Carlisle United (h)	2-2	Nish, Glover	20,809
Sept 2	Bristol City (h)	4-0	Farrington, Kellard, Brown, Nish (pen)	20,228
Sept 5	Oxford United (a)	0-1		12,895
Sept 12	Luton Town (h)	1-0	Brown	24,226
Sept 19	Charlton Athletic (a)	1-0	Partridge	10,940
Sept 26	Portsmouth (h)	2-0	Glover, Farrington	25,613
Sept 30	Middlesbrough (h)	3-2	Brown 2, Kellard	26,279
Oct 3	Blackburn Rovers (a)	2-2	Partridge, Nish (pen)	9,061
Oct 10	Sunderland (h)	1-0	Glover	26,580
Oct 17	Cardiff City (a)	2-2	Farrington, Sjoberg	26,008
Oct 20	Birmingham City (a)	0-0		25,381
Oct 24	Sheffield Wednesday (a)	3-0	Brown, Nish 2 (1 pen)	23,160
Oct 31	Bolton Wanderers (h)	1-0	Kellard	24,485
Nov 7	Watford (a)	1-0	Nish (pen)	17,107
Nov 14	Swindon Town (h)	3-1	Jones og, Harland og, Brown	26,063
Nov 21	Norwich City (a)	2-2	Manley, Farrington	16,774
Nov 28	Orient (h)	4-0	Brown 2, Manley, Kellard	23,699
Dec 5	Hull City (a)	0-3		21,210
Dec 12	Millwall (h)	2-1	Kellard, Fern	22,062
Dec 19	QPR (h)	0-0		23,865
Dec 26	Sheffield United (a)	1-2	Farrington	31,843
Jan 9	Middlesbrough (a)	0-1		30,652
Jan 16	Birmingham City (h)	1-4	Sjoberg	25,657
Feb 6	Hull City (h)	0-0		30,744
Feb 20	Norwich City (h)	2-1	Fern, Partridge	24,866
Feb 27	Bolton Wanderers (a)	3-0	Sjoberg 2, Brown	8,362
Mar 1	Millwall (a)	0-0		10,738
Mar 10	Sheffield Wednesday (h)	1-0	Brown	25,843
Mar 13	Swindon Town (a)	1-0	Kellard	17,979
Mar 20	Watford (h)	1-1	Nish	24,817
Mar 27	Oxford United (h)	0-0		22,233
Mar 29	Orient (a)	1-0	Glover	12,736
Apr 3	Carlisle United (a)	1-0	Brown	15,325
Apr 10	Sheffield United (h)	0-0		36,752
Apr 12	Luton Town (a)	3-1	Manley, Farrington, Brown	24.405
Apr 13	Blackburn Rovers (h)	1-1	Carlin	32,749
Apr 17	Sunderland (a)	0-0		17,353
Apr 24	Charlton Athletic (h)	1-0	Went og	29,121
Apr 27	Bristol City (a)	1-0	Brown	16,103
May 1	Portsmouth (a)	2-1	Farrington, Brown	18,795

LEAGUE CUP

Sept 9	Southampton (h)	3-2	Farrington, Glover, Fern	20,728
Oct 7	Bolton Wanderers (a)	1-1	Farrington	8,623
Oct 14	Bolton Wanderers (h)	1-0	Sjoberg	18,068
Oct 28	Bristol City (h)	2-2	Farrington, Nish (pen)	21,577
Nov 3	Bristol City (a)	1-2 aet	Nish (pen)	16,575

FA CUP

Jan 2	Notts County (h)	2-0	Partridge, Brown	33,770
Jan 25	Torquay United (h)	3-0	Glover, Partridge, Cross	27,263
Feb 13	Oxford United (h)	1-1	Partridge	34,802
Feb 17	Oxford United (a)	3-1 aet	Fern 2, Brown	17,948
Mar 6	Arsenal (h)	0-0		42,000
Mat 15	Arsenal (a)	0-1		57,443

It was while I was at Leicester that I also got to know Reggie Kray. I got a call from whoever was in charge of liaising with prisoners at Leicester Prison, where a maximum security wing had been constructed. He told me they wanted to keep the long-

One of Reggie Kray's letters to Frank from Parkhurst prison.

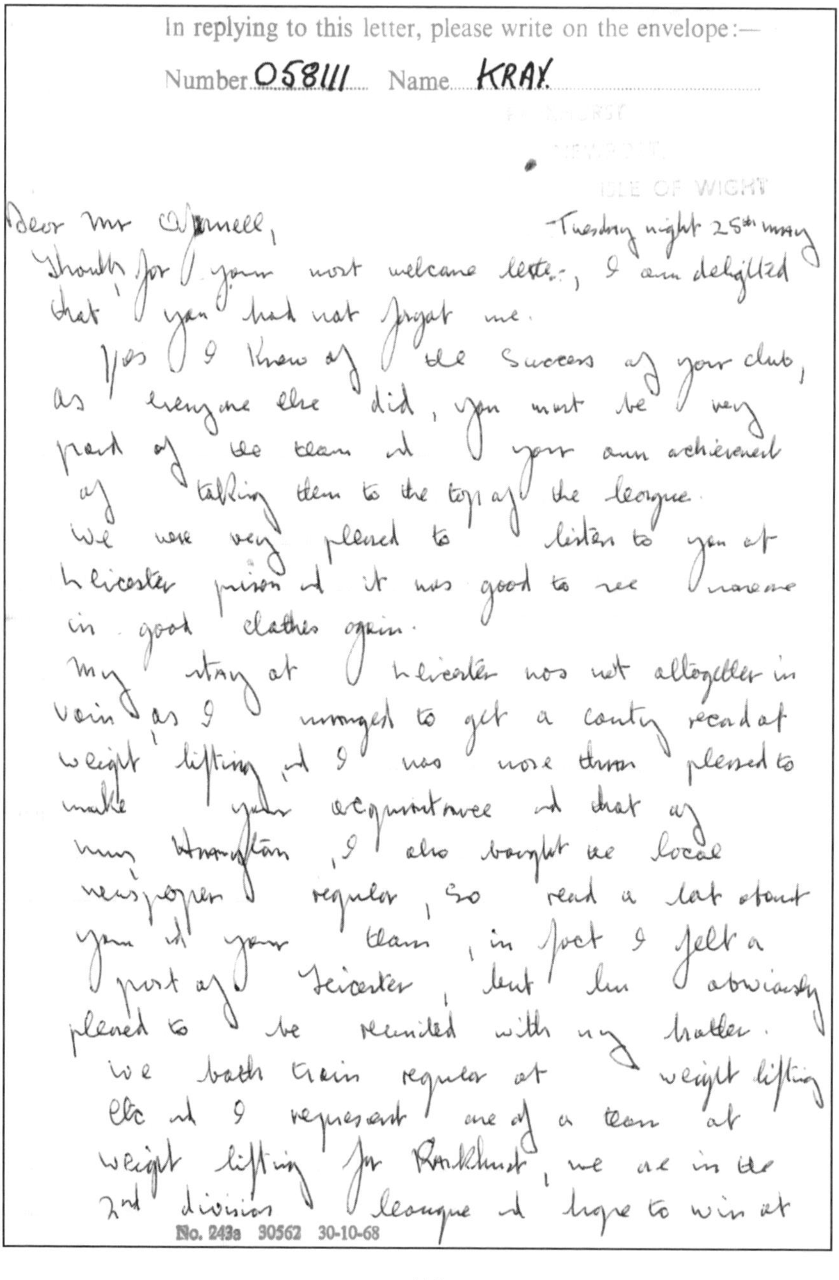

In replying to this letter, please write on the envelope:—

Number 058111   Name KRAY

PARKHURST
ISLE OF WIGHT

Dear Mr O'Donnell,   Tuesday night 25th May

Thank you for your most welcome letter, I am delighted that you had not forgot me.

Yes I knew of the success of your club, as everyone else did, you must be very proud of the team and your own achievement of taking them to the top of the league. We were very pleased to listen to you at Leicester prison and it was good to see someone in good clothes again.

My stay at Leicester was not altogether in vain as I managed to get a county record at weight lifting and I was more than pleased to make your acquaintance and that of your Brampton, I also bought the local newspaper regular, so read a lot about you and your team, in fact I felt a part of Leicester, but I'm obviously pleased to be reunited with my brother. We both train regular at weight lifting etc and I represent one of a team at weight lifting for Parkhurst, we are in the 2nd division league and hope to win at

No. 243a   90562   30-10-68

term inmates interested in outside subjects and aware of what was going on in the world. They had built a new gym at the prison and he asked whether I was prepared to go in one Sunday a month and talk about how the players prepared and how they kept fit.

I'd done some prison visiting at Dartmoor when I was at Torquay - I had been approached by the Catholic chaplain to visit Catholic prisoners - and I said I would be pleased to help out. I suppose it was my Catholic background to practise charitable deeds.

Maybe some managers do it now and you don't hear about it. I certainly never said anything publicly about it at the time. So I went into this room at Leicester Prison and there were about six or seven prisoners there, and I knew Reg was one of them. His brother Ron was also in Leicester at the time but he wouldn't take part. You could tell Reg was the boss, but he was very polite.

I went into different types of training, things like weight training and relevant exercises, which would be appropriate for them in a confined space, and the talks lasted about an hour. At the end Reg would always come up to me and thank me for coming. On one occasion, he told me what a nice suit I was wearing - he said it reminded him of when he was on the outside and used to wear Savile Row suits!

He was later moved to Parkhurst on the Isle of Wight and I went to visit him there as well. That's when I talked to him as an individual. He admitted he had done wrong and deserved his punishment but that he wasn't all bad and had done some good things in his time. He came out with his life story, telling me about his mother and his upbringing. I quoted him what the Psalmist said "Man judges by appearances but God looks into the heart and he knows what good you've done." It must have affected him because he used to send me Christmas cards saying: 'God bless, Frank'.

I enjoyed my time at Leicester. John Smith was a very efficient club secretary and his secretary, June Davis, was a delightful lady. In fact all the staff were very helpful, including Gladys and the tea ladies.

Everybody was so welcoming - there was nothing about Leicester City Football Club you could dislike.

EVENTS OF 1971

The UK and Ireland switched to decimal currency.

Intel released the world's first microprocessor.

The BBC launched the Open University.

Walt Disney World opened in Florida.

Arsenal completed the League and FA Cup double.

**Frank O'Farrell succeeded Matt Busby as manager of
Manchester United.**

5

A NICE DAY FOR AN EXECUTION

It was the best of times,
It was the worst of times ...
It was the season of light,
It was the season of darkness.

Charles Dickens

WE WERE back in Division One, but I felt the Leicester board were being a bit mean on the new deal they were offering me as my original contract was up. I had spoken to Brian Clough about it and he said ask for £10,000 a year. He didn't tell me what he was getting, but he said £10,000 was fair. I did all my own negotiating and I was offered £10,000, but there was an issue over bonuses. I would have willingly agreed the right deal and stayed, and I certainly wasn't contemplating leaving the club, but then Manchester United came in for me.

It started with a phone call from Matt Gillies, who I had succeeded as Leicester manager. He said he'd had a call from Matt Busby and that he was only telling me and no-one else, and he asked me would I speak with them. As I had not yet agreed a new contract with Leicester, I felt there was no harm in talking to Matt so I said yes.

He phoned me shortly after and said he wanted to meet me somewhere without people knowing. I said I was in London at the weekend but he said he didn't want to risk meeting there just in case anyone saw us and it got into the newspapers.

He didn't have to spell it out that he wanted to discuss the possibility of me becoming their new manager - it was obvious. After the meetings in London I was on my way back up to Leicester - I think it was for David Nish's wedding - and I had agreed to meet Matt in a lay-by just off the M1 at the Leicester

115

turn off. I gave him directions to meet at a certain time. I was there and a car pulled in behind me.

I said follow me and we'll go to my house. I think he had a Mercedes but I can't remember what I had, possibly a Ford. We parked a little bit up the road from my house. He got into my car and once we got to the house, I said just go up the steps and Ann will let you in. I will park the car in the garage.

Ann had put the girls in the lounge, said I was having a guest and didn't want to be disturbed. But as Matt went past the window, one of them saw him and said "That's Matt Busby. I've seen him on the television - perhaps Daddy is going to sign George Best." That's the reason she thought he had come to see me!

So we had a talk. He told me he was retiring, that he had let things go - he freely admitted that - and that there was quite a lot of work to be done and they wanted me to be manager. They were

Receiving the Texaco-sponsored Irish Sports Personality of the Year award from Ireland Prime Minister Jack Lynch in 1971. Lynch was a former hurler and an early hero of Frank's.

Frank pictured with wife Ann and daughters Catherine and Bernadette. Frank is now a grandfather to six (Bernadette, who now lives in Essex, has three boys, and Catherine, who is still in Devon, has two boys and a girl). Frank is also a great grandfather to seven-year-old Callum Francis, the son of Catherine's eldest boy, Richard.

offering a five-year contract, and he said it would take that time to sort things out. He mentioned the bonuses if United were to win the League or FA Cup, but the important thing was that the salary was £12,000. I said I'd think it over during the weekend. He said he'd approached Len Shipman to see if he could talk to me and Len had said no, that I wasn't interested in the Manchester United job.

I had never said that and I was a bit put out as it just wasn't true. Obviously we hadn't agreed a new contract so Len had panicked, and saw himself in a bit of bother. So I said to Matt I'd think it over and talk to my chairman on Monday. The chairman's son lived two doors down from me and I was worried he was going to see Matt coming and going. But he got off and only my two daughters had seen him. I have to say I was quite chuffed to be asked to manage Manchester United. It hadn't been that long since I had been manager at Weymouth and here I was being offered the job as manager of one of the biggest clubs in the game. It is not something I ever envisaged as you can't plan who you are going to manage. You can only do your best and hope that the work you do gets noticed by bigger clubs.

On the Monday I said to Len Shipman "Mr Chairman, I'd like to have a word with you." I said I understand Manchester United have made an approach for me. I didn't say I had already met with Matt, and he said "Oh yes, their chairman rang me this morning." But Matt Busby had told me he had talked to Len down in London.

I said I'd like to talk to them and he said he would ring them. I said no, I'll ring them. I rang Matt and made an appointment to meet him at a convenient place for both of us called the Mackworth Hotel on the road that goes across to Manchester from Derby. We agreed to meet on the Tuesday in the pub car park.

Shortly after I arrived at the pub, a Rolls Royce came in with Louis Edwards, the Manchester United chairman, driving and Matt sat in the back. There were a few other cars in the car park and I went over to say hello. Matt said there were too many cars around and someone might see us. So I said I'll get back in my car and they should follow me and we'll find some place down the road.

I saw a B road off the main road - I didn't know where it was going to lead us - and there was a farmhouse across the way and a lay-by so I pulled into the lay-by and the Rolls Royce pulled in behind me. I got out and went to the car, and Matt introduced me properly to Louis Edwards. They asked whether I had come to a decision and I said to Matt "Could you repeat the terms again?" Matt said it was a five-year contract with a salary of £12,000 plus bonuses. That was the same as he had offered me on the Saturday but Louis interrupted and said "No Matt you've got that wrong - the salary is £15,000."

Matt apologised that he had got it wrong but I think our whole relationship was damaged from that moment onwards. I felt something wasn't right and Matt knew that I knew he had tried to cheat me.

It certainly left a bad taste, and a few years later, after I had left the club, I was talking to Jimmy Murphy (who had worked behind the scenes at Old Trafford for many years as coach, assistant manager and chief scout) and he said he knew the story to be true because Matt told him he could've got Frank for £12,000 but "that big stupid bugger told him it was £15,000." They were Jimmy's own words.

Why Matt would not want to offer me what he had been instructed to by his board of directors I'll never know. Perhaps he didn't want anyone to get what he was getting. Or perhaps he wanted to go back to Louis Edwards and tell him I got Frank for £12,000 a year rather than £15,000.

All the same Manchester United were the best club in the country, and their history was part of the fabric of the nation. The tragedy at Munich in 1958 had an effect on people and they were a lot of people's favourite club. I actually passed my driving test in Preston on the day of the Munich disaster and remember vividly seeing the newspaper placards around the town.

Matt said he was going to be a director, that he'd done his bit and was happy to hand it over. There was no talk of him being any sort of managing director and supervising the manager. That didn't come into it and I certainly wouldn't have taken the job on that basis.

I was a little hurt that some people felt I had let Leicester down in leaving them after guiding them back to Division One. I felt I had done my duty in getting them promoted and it is not as if I went after the Manchester United job. To be honest it is probably the only job I would have left Leicester for, and the Leicester directors knew that.

Ann and I stayed in a hotel in Manchester for a while and we were recommended to live in Sale in Cheshire. But my first priority was my wife and children. It might seem crazy these days but we needed a house near a bus stop as Ann couldn't drive and she needed to get to the shops and church when I was at work. Also the girls could then catch a bus to school. In the end we got a house in Eccles Old Road, Salford, and it was a lovely house. People said I should not have gone there but I knew where Ann and I wanted to live.

The girls went to a convent school in Salford and Buile Hill Park was on the other side of the road. It was a nice area and Ann

Matt Busby welcomes Frank to Old Trafford in July 1971.

could walk up to the church for Mass during the week. She was happy in the house and she could cope with the things she had to do while I was away. We paid £16,000 for the house and later sold it for £32,000 when we moved back to Devon. That was big money in those days.

I was very impressed with Old Trafford, but who wouldn't have been? It was the top job in football, everything was bigger, from the size of the crowds to the players. It was a totally different level to what I had been used to. Once again I asked Malcolm Musgrove to come with me. It was a step-up for him too.

I struck up a good relationship with the players to start with. I had played in the First Division myself with Preston and I think that was important. They were listening to someone who'd played at their level. I had actually played against both Denis Law and Bobby Charlton while at Preston.

Denis and I had a chat early on and he asked to play as a midfielder as he had played in that position on a pre-season tour to Switzerland. I dismissed it straight away. I don't know if he wanted an easier life in midfield as he'd been a striker for a long time and taken a lot of knocks. In a polite way I said it was not going to happen and he was OK about it - there were no issues.

I inherited the contracts when I joined United, and it wasn't easy to make changes. But I got a list of all the wages and I discovered George Best wasn't the best paid player, so I made him the best paid. I can't remember whether Bobby or Denis was the highest paid but I looked at George's wages and told him he should be on more. I thought it was only fair as he was the best player at the club. He was quite pleased but subsequently it didn't make any difference to his attitude. But it was right for me to have done it - and it should have been done before I arrived. I didn't dispute any of the wages, but I felt George should have been on more. They were on around £125 to £150 per week at the time.

When I first arrived at the club, Old Trafford was closed because of crowd trouble at the Stretford End and we had to play our first four League games away from home. We lost my first game, 2-1 in a pre-season Watney Cup tie (a competition for the top two scoring sides in each division who had not been promoted or gained a place in Europe) at Third Division Halifax Town, with Willie Morgan missing a penalty, and then we had to play the first two League 'home' games at other grounds - Arsenal at Anfield and West Brom at Stoke City.

It took a lot of organising to get the two games sorted at different venues, but Bill Shankly at Liverpool was especially good in helping out, and it made me realise just how many friends United had in the game. At one stage I even contacted Wembley Stadium with a view to playing the Arsenal game there, and while the Wembley authorities were really helpful, they were unable to accommodate us because they still had speedway running at the stadium.

Because of the crowd trouble at Old Trafford, which had involved a knife being thrown onto the pitch, I put an appeal in the programme for the fans to behave and not use bad language. They responded quite well and I put a 'thank you' up on the board at the ground.

We won both the first two 'home' games 3-1, having kicked off the League programme with a 2-2 draw at Derby County and a 3-2 win at Chelsea, so we had made a promising start. George scored a hat-trick in a 4-2 home win over West Ham, and again in a 5-2 win at Southampton and we lost only two of our first 23 League matches, 1-0 defeats at Everton and at home to Leeds United.

We led the table by five points at one stage and we were still top at Christmas when Matt Busby said in the Daily Mirror that "Frank O'Farrell was the best signing I ever made."

DIVISION ONE TABLE on December 4, 1971

	P	W	D	L	F	A	W	D	L	F	A	Pts
Manchester United	20	9	0	1	23	10	5	4	1	23	14	32
Derby County	20	6	4	0	23	8	4	3	3	12	8	27
Manchester City	20	8	1	1	24	6	3	4	3	13	14	27
Leeds United	20	8	3	0	21	5	4	0	5	9	12	27
Sheffield United	20	6	3	1	24	8	5	0	5	12	18	25
Liverpool	20	7	2	0	18	9	3	3	5	9	11	25
Tottenham Hotspur	20	9	2	0	29	7	0	4	5	8	18	24
Arsenal	20	6	0	3	17	8	4	2	5	12	17	22
Chelsea	20	5	3	2	19	12	3	3	4	8	12	22
Wolverhampton Wand.	20	6	5	0	25	14	2	1	6	9	17	22
Stoke City	20	5	2	2	13	7	3	3	5	9	15	21
Ipswich Town	20	4	5	2	10	8	1	4	4	6	15	19
West Ham United	20	5	3	3	12	8	1	3	5	7	11	18
Coventry City	20	4	5	1	13	10	1	3	6	9	23	18
Everton	20	6	2	3	17	7	0	3	6	4	13	17
Leicester City	20	3	4	3	8	6	2	3	5	13	19	17
Huddersfield Town	21	4	2	4	10	12	2	2	7	9	19	16
Southampton	20	4	2	3	15	14	2	1	8	10	30	15
Newcastle United	20	4	3	3	13	10	0	3	7	7	21	14
Crystal Palace	20	3	2	5	14	16	1	2	7	5	20	12
Nottingham Forest	21	2	2	6	14	18	1	3	7	12	25	11
West Bromwich Albion	20	1	2	6	6	11	2	3	6	8	16	11

Frank and long-time friend Malcolm Musgrove (above) and Frank with Louis Edwards and Matt Busby (below). In Frank's first season in charge at Old Trafford, Busby said: "I look upon Frank as my last great signing ... possibly the greatest of the lot. I think he will make a huge success of this great club of ours. He has a way with him - a presence if you like. He has a personality that strikes you, a quality that convinces you he knows what he is doing. He's got everything a manager needs and most important of all the respect of the players." A year later Busby looked on without saying a word when Frank's contract was terminated.

I was getting on well enough with Matt and Louis Edwards, though Louis was very dependent on Matt and was not happy unless he was near by. I never socialised with them, but board meetings were OK.

Despite being top of the table, the team was ageing a little. I hadn't come in looking to change things overnight, but there hadn't been much rebuilding done, and only Sammy McIlroy came through the youth policy at the time.

Sammy was 17 when I gave him his debut in a derby match against Manchester City that finished in a thrilling 3-3 draw. He was a very confident lad and scored on what was a very good debut. It was good to see him managing at Macclesfield and Morecambe in recent years, and it would have been nice had that been a platform for Sammy to manage at a higher level one day, even if that seems to be getting ever more difficult with the number of foreign managers being employed in England.

The United players had a kind of a mind set. I can remember one particular phrase they used to say "let's play the football", which was a kind of vague concept. I also heard the comment that "if we get one, we'll get four" because that was the way they played, very much off the cuff. They weren't an easy side to bring up to speed with the modern game and tactics. They felt they were free spirits, and none of them became successful managers. Bobby Charlton was given an opportunity at Preston but even he found it difficult.

It was never going to be easy bringing in new players and I knew I would have to bide my time. It was also going to be difficult to follow in Matt's footsteps, a bit like following Lord Olivier on the stage, but Matt had said I had five years to turn things around and I felt that was more than enough time to do the job. Disappointingly Matt didn't support me while I tried to do it.

We needed to bolster the defence, and though Steve James was a young player coming through and did well for a while, you could look at the defence and find failings in a lot of them. David Sadler wasn't a natural defender, and the centre of defence was a position that needed strengthening.

I signed Martin Buchan from Aberdeen and Matt said he was pleased that changes were finally being made. Martin used to go home after training and play his guitar, he didn't go out socialising

Deep in thought with Malcolm Musgrove during a summer training session. Pictured either side of them are Bobby Charlton and Denis Law.

or to nightclubs and I feel he was slightly resented because of it.

Later, in my second season when we lost 4-1 at home to Spurs, Matt blamed Martin for one of the goals. He was interfering and undermining me.

He told Danny Blanchflower he was a junior director but in truth he was far from being that. Matt had such a massive influence on the club and the chairman couldn't move without him.

Matt had let the team grow old, and unlike say Bill Shankly at Liverpool, he had failed to make changes when needed. Shanks did it brilliantly, moving players on and giving them testimonials. He was great like that. Matt should have done the same, but he didn't want to fall out with players who had been loyal to him. He brought other people in to do that - including me - and then didn't back them.

It's a fact that whenever a new manager goes to a club some players feel they're under threat. If you are going to build a new team, it's obvious some players will have to leave. I can understand that feeling as I was a player myself. Managers don't usually make changes on a whim, it is because performances are not up to the required standard.

During our good start to the 1971-72 season, we tried a different formation, 4-4-2, with Alan Gowling playing as a midfield player who could defend and protect the centre-backs and also prove useful at corners.

He had been signed as a centre-forward but I had Law and Best up front and I felt Alan, who had a terrific motor, would make a good central midfield player as he had the height to head goal kicks forward, and he could get on the end of crosses as well. It worked well and his performances played a big part in the way we started the season.

Pat Crerand thought he had a bit more in him but I wasn't going to bring him back and I said the decision was made. I took advice from two people I trusted, John Aston, the chief scout, and Jimmy Murphy, both of whom said he was past his best.

I also made sure that the physio, Laurie Brown, got all the equipment he was looking for. It surprised me he didn't have it as the physiotherapist is such an important figure in a club and I wanted the best equipment possible to deal with injured players.

To begin with George played out of his skin. He was absolutely brilliant. He had his weaknesses but he was genuinely a very likeable man. He was engaging, witty, cheerful and with the gift of the gab. When he was at the club he was no trouble at all - he always played and trained very hard. But when he was away from the club, that was when the trouble started.

He was also the best player I ever managed and it is a pity he never got the chance to show his talents on the biggest stage of all, at the World Cup finals.

My priority was to keep George playing at his best for as long as I could, and try and keep him on the straight and narrow. I often used to get phone calls as I was going to bed telling me George had done this or done that. His life outside the club wasn't good. He was living in a big house in Cheshire all alone and I was looking for a solution to that.

He lived with Pat Crerand and his wife for a while. Pat offered to put him up, trying to be helpful, which was very kind of him, but it was no answer. George was still getting himself into some scrapes. His habits were already formed by the time I got to Old Trafford and it was something I took on. Matt had signed him as a boy and he couldn't handle him, so what chance did I have? He had a wayward manner and was always threatening to give the game up. In May 1972, at the end of my first season, he announced while in Spain that he was going to quit football - he was just 26 at the time.

The other players would moan when George failed to turn up for training and I would punish him with fines, but it was only a slap on the wrist. He hinted at times that Manchester United didn't need a new manager, they needed new players and he was right. I think he was concerned that the United team was not good enough.

He also did an interview on Michael Parkinson's show soon after I was appointed. It was mainly about his lifestyle, and I didn't think it was appropriate, or a good thing to have done. Parkinson was highlighting something we were trying to deal with - George's complicated private life - and I wrote to Parky telling him I thought it was inappropriate. I didn't get a reply.

When I had him in my office on one occasion trying to fathom out what his problems were and to see if I could give him guidance in any way, George said he was worried about his parents in Belfast. It was during the IRA bombing campaign and I said I was prepared to go to the board of directors and ask if it would be feasible, and if they would agree, to buy a house in Manchester to rent to George's parents, and where George would live with them. It would mean his fears for their safety would be allayed and he could also be subject to some supervision in a home environment.

George agreed it would be a good arrangement, the directors were willing to go along with the idea and I was given permission to go to Belfast when it was convenient to do so and discuss the proposal with George's parents. But George wasn't to know about the visit.

I flew to Dublin on the pretence of watching a game there. I caught the Belfast train from Dublin and got a taxi from the station to George's parents' house. I found them to be very pleasant people who were also worried about George. They were grateful

Frank and George Best leave the FA enquiry at Lancaster Gate called to rule on Best allegedly swearing at a referee in the 3-2 win at Chelsea. Willie Morgan (pictured next to Frank in the taxi below) gave evidence on Best's behalf and Best escaped a ban when he insisted he had sworn at Morgan and not the referee.

to me for trying to help their son, and they were supportive of my suggestion. But they said they would have to try and secure the council house in which they were living so that it could be passed on to their daughter. The whole idea looked promising if George was being truthful with us.

When I returned to Old Trafford on the Friday morning, George was not there, and Malcolm Musgrove said he had not been at training all week. Malcolm said they had a phone call to say George was visiting his parents in Belfast - which I knew was a complete lie!

I decided I could not select him to play against Wolverhampton Wanderers on the Saturday, and I told the other players that George had been dropped, and now it was up to them to prove they could win without him. Well, they couldn't win without him, and we were beaten 3-1 at home by Wolverhampton Wanderers.

The weekend press, knowing what had taken place, were very critical of George and rightly so. The daily press continued the criticism, asking me whether George would be playing at Southampton in the FA Cup the following weekend. When

Frank is about to inform the Manchester United players of his decision to drop the wayward George Best.

George showed up on the Monday morning, he accepted the dressing down I gave him, and trained hard all week. I picked him to play at Southampton and we got a 1-1 draw at The Dell, with a replay at Old Trafford on the Wednesday.

The press hung on to the story and were still giving him stick. In the replay the score was 0-0 in the second half when George produced two moments of brilliance to score twice. He celebrated by going over towards the press box and giving two V signs to the occupants. We won the game 4-1. In the end nothing came of George's parents moving to Manchester.

George also asked me on one occasion if he could draw his pension out. He must have been short of money and maybe in debt. I told him I would not have it on my conscience to approve such an idea as I thought with the way he was living, he might need that pension in the years ahead.

You were always on edge with George, never knowing whether he was going to turn up and if he did, whether he would then get sent off. He was sent off in one of my early matches against Chelsea at Stamford Bridge for allegedly swearing at the referee, though he maintained it was directed at a fellow player. He was summoned to London to answer the charges made against him by the Football Association, and Willie Morgan went as a witness as he was the nearest player when the incident occurred. The verdict went in favour of George, though from what I can recall the referee was not best pleased.

Bobby Charlton was captain of the team and we'd practise different free-kicks on the training ground. Then George would see something else during games, try it and might mess it up. Bobby would come in complaining afterwards but I told him he was the captain, he had 100 international caps so he could sort it out on the pitch.

I used to get angry as Bobby was a bit of a moaner. He also sulked when I left him out of the team for a couple of games. Nobody has a divine right to be picked every week and I felt we were weak in midfield, and were struggling to break up the opposition attacks. I moved Martin Buchan into midfield, and Bobby wasn't happy at all.

There was then the threat that George was going to get shot when we played away at Newcastle United. The team coach got broken into and the police took it quite seriously and gave him an escort. One of the other players said to George to move around a bit faster so to dodge the bullets!

I felt we had a great chance of winning the title, especially if George continued playing at his best. But then he started going missing, culminating with him flying to Spain and announcing he was retiring. I was asked by the press if I was going after him. I said "No blooming way".

A lot of the senior players had a close relationship with Matt Busby, even playing golf with him, and they'd take their gripes to him. I suspect he would be saying he would have done things differently, and I didn't feel that was a healthy situation.

I once made Denis Law substitute and he didn't want to sit on the bench and watch the game, he wanted to stay in the dressing room. I said you'd better sit on the bench so you know what's happening. If he wasn't active in the game, he wasn't interested.

I also left Brian Kidd out of the side early on in my time at Old Trafford and there was a picture of him in the paper playing golf on the Friday before the game. That was out of order as there was a rule that you couldn't play golf after Wednesday in the week in the build-up to matches. But we smoothed things over and Brian did a good job for the team, playing in several different positions.

I had been used to talking any problems through with the chairman at my previous clubs. Louis Edwards had a food company that supplied school dinners, and though he wasn't always the best at putting his case across, I got on with him and I had no reason to dislike him.

I never had a big transfer fund at United, but before I went to negotiate, I used to know what price I could pay. If I was chasing a player or wanted to make a signing, I'd always liaise with the chairman and things would be talked about. But every time I talked to Louis about something, he would then speak to Matt, who would give his view about any possible deal. It was an impossible position for me to be in.

There had also been the problem with the manager's office when I first arrived at Old Trafford. Matt was still in the office and there were workmen constructing a new small office for the new manager - me - down the corridor. The alarm bells started ringing again. Matt was not manager anymore, but he was still going to keep the manager's office.

I was uneasy with that and I am not one to keep my feelings in check, though I always did things politely. I thought it was an important issue to resolve, especially regarding what the press would say, and I said to him I felt it would not look right if he continued to occupy what was seen as the manager's office.

It was nothing to do with having a big office, but it was the manager's office and I was the manager. I said he should have the new office, not me. He thought about it for a minute or two and then said he would move his stuff out.

What with the salary issue as well, it meant that I didn't get off on the right note with Matt from the start. If there is no trust, then there is nothing.

When we played at Leicester in my first season, we went into the hotel bar before lunch for a quick drink and Louis said "Frank I'm very pleased the way we've started, you can have another £50 per month in expenses". I didn't take it, I said I'm well paid and happy with the money, though I do appreciate the gesture. He said Matt had carte blanche to sign for anything, even his groceries and anything from the club shop!

Things tailed off after our good start and after Christmas we suffered seven straight defeats, including a 5-1 loss at Leeds United and home defeats to Wolves, Chelsea and Newcastle United. George had started to disappear and to be honest, we were probably a one-man team at times. Even when George wasn't at his best, he would distract the opposition and leave openings for other players.

When he was on top form, George was virtually unstoppable. Like when he scored that famous solo goal against Sheffield United at Old Trafford that was on Match of the Day. That was just brilliant.

I tried to be fair with George but at one stage I'd have lost my credibility with the other players had I continued to play him when he wasn't coming to training. You do what's morally right, even if you have to suffer the consequences, and that's what I did.

As a player George was on a par with the likes of Pele, Tom Finney and Stanley Matthews, apart from his reliability. Pele was

Manchester United in 1972-73. Back (left to right): John Fitzpatrick, Tony Middle: Malcolm Musgrove (coach), Steve James, David Sadler, Alex Frank O'Farrell (manager). Front: Willie Morgan, Ian Storey-Moore, Deni

Young, Tommy O'Neil, Sammy McIlroy, Carlo Sartori, Tony Dunne.
Stepney, John Connaughton, Jimmy Rimmer, Brian Kidd, Martin Buchan,
Law, George Best, Bobby Charlton.

a very professional man - he respected the game and did what was expected of him - and Tom and Stan were the same. They didn't abuse their bodies and while Tom played into his 40s, Stan played professionally when he was 50. George was all but finished at 27, but was he better on the day? It's a very difficult call - he certainly had all the attributes. His lifestyle caught up with him and you can't treat your body like he did and stay the course as a professional footballer.

The team was poorer for George not being in it, and I tried my utmost to keep him playing. There was an awful lot to admire about George's ability, and it is sad in one respect that his career and life went like it did. But you make your own choices in life and take responsibility for your own actions.

As a manager you have to be judged on your own team, not

Ted MacDougall joins Manchester United. Frank later admitted that the United players refused to "accept" the striker bought from Bournemouth for £200,000.

one you have inherited off someone else. You stand and fall by the team you have created, but I never got that chance at Old Trafford. If I'd have stayed at that club I don't think they would have been relegated to Division Two like they were.

I signed Ian Storey-Moore as a replacement for George, though only after he had been kidnapped by Brian Clough. I was in the middle of negotiations with Nottingham Forest manager Matt Gillies when Ian was called away. We'd all met at a hotel and we couldn't find him anywhere.

Apparently Cloughie had called him and he had gone, and Matt was outraged by such behaviour. His wife didn't know where he was - it was a real mystery. He ended up being paraded before a Derby County home game as a new signing and I was furious. But in the end we got it sorted and he did join us and not Derby.

I know some of the other players reckoned Ian was injury prone, but I don't think they were welcoming of any new players at the time because they saw them as a threat.

Though we picked up towards the end of the season, we finally finished eighth, with Brian Clough's Derby County crowned champions. We lost to Stoke in both cup competitions, losing in replays in the Fourth Round of the League Cup (a second replay) and the Sixth Round of the FA Cup.

With George out of the equation for much of the time, our goalscoring record was pretty awful so I brought in Ted MacDougall and Wyn Davies. Ted, though he had been playing for Bournemouth in Division Three, was one of the leading scorers in the League and had famously netted nine times in an FA Cup tie against Margate the previous season.

I bought him for £200,000 - Bournemouth were managed by my former West Ham team-mate John Bond at the time - and it was a bit of a gamble. He scored four goals in his first 11 games which was good in a struggling team, but I always felt he wasn't accepted by the other players. They had prejudices from the start about the way he played. He was not one of their sort and he got the cold shoulder.

There was a clause in Ted's contract that Bournemouth would get a bonus if he scored 20 goals, but United got rid of him before that happened after I had left the club.

As for Wyn, he wasn't in the same class as Best or Law, but he was good in the air. But there was of sort of general feeling around the club that "he can't play". Law, Best and Charlton were on their way out and something had to be done, and it needed an outsider to have an objective view. I don't think there was anything personal in it, but people seemed opposed to me making changes.

I also talked to the board about signing Alan Ball and Peter Shilton, but there was a shortage of money and Leicester wouldn't sell Shilton at the time anyway. Ball was discussed but he ended up going to Arsenal. Had we signed Shilton, I am convinced I wouldn't have been sacked so soon.

Alex Stepney was a good goalkeeper but in certain key games he wasn't quite as commanding as he should have been. He let in a soft goal against Leeds United, and he made mistakes that Shilton would never have made, but to be honest I didn't see it as a priority at the time.

We didn't make a good start to my second season in charge, losing our first three games, at home to Ipswich (1-2) and away at Liverpool and Everton (both 0-2) and not winning until we beat Derby County 3-0 at Old Trafford in our tenth game.

After we lost 4-1 at home to Spurs in the October, the club held a dinner for the staff and Ann and I went. It was a pleasant evening, though it would have been nicer if we'd won the match, and on the way home in the car Ann said Matt had had a word with her and said "Your husband is an independent sod and you should get him to come and talk to me."

I felt that was atrocious, passing messages through my wife. I would see him often enough around the ground and he could have come and talked to me and told me he wasn't happy about things rather than discuss it with Ann. She didn't get involved with football - she was at home with the children - and I thought it was way out of order.

So on the Monday morning I waited for Matt to come in - he came in most mornings - and we're having our morning cuppa and I said "Ann said you said I'm an independent sod and I should come and talk to you. Well here I am." I was polite about it and he started finding fault, first with Martin Buchan.

He said Buchan isn't playing well (I'd signed him and

eventually he became a great player and captain of the club) and I said the team isn't playing well. He wouldn't accept that and he said Martin had been at fault for the first goal against Spurs on the Saturday. I had to tell him he had got it wrong and the goal hadn't happened the way he described it.

I asked him what else did he want to say? I had also dropped Bobby Charlton, a big decision, and he said "I don't think you should have dropped Bobby" - now that was interfering. If he was saying things like that to Bobby, no wonder Bobby didn't like me!

I suppose if Matt had studied Irish history he might have learned that Cork people can be very independent. In the course of the city's history, some have been prepared to pay the ultimate price for it.

On March 20, 1920, Tomas McCurtain, Cork's first republican Lord Mayor, was shot and killed by British forces in front of his wife and children. His funeral was one of the largest ever in Cork. Terence McSwiney was elected unanimously to succeed McCurtain as Lord Mayor and was sentenced to two years incarceration in Brixton Prison. He went on hunger strike following his sentence for 73 days and died in extreme agony. He wrote "Victory is won not by those who can inflict the most, but by those who can endure the most."

Matt questioned my decisions and created discontent. I didn't feel he had been honest with me from the outset, and in the end it made my job untenable. He wasn't the manager but he couldn't let go and he became a real hindrance.

They sacked me during Christmas week and treated me abominably. I had gone through bad patches before at other clubs, and most managers have dips during the season.

We had started to pick up some results, and had won three of our previous five games, but we were again without George for the trip to face Crystal Palace at Selhurst Park on December 16, and Bobby Charlton was also out injured.

Ian Storey-Moore hit the post early on, and had that gone in things might have been different. But we were beaten 5-0 by a Palace side who were bottom of the table.

Tommy Docherty was there in the crowd watching the game. I didn't see him but I heard he was there, though he was manager of the Scottish national team at the time. I found out after the game that he had been sounded out as to whether he would be available should I be sacked the following week.

On the Tuesday (December 19) I had a phone call in the morning and was told there was a board meeting. John Aston had also been called in to the meeting and he picked me up in his car. It was a lovely sunny morning and I remarked to John that "it was a nice day for an execution." I didn't imagine for one minute that John would be sacked at the same time. Malcolm Musgrove was also summoned to the meeting and he travelled on his own to Old Trafford. He too was sacked.

I went into the meeting prepared. The press had been speculating at the weekend about my future and the night before I had been to a party to celebrate Bobby Charlton's testimonial, and I wasn't even seated on the top table. I had helped to arrange the testimonial so I knew something was up. Bobby had tried to get Benfica over but they couldn't come so I contacted Jock Stein who said he'd bring Celtic down for a fee, though Matt wasn't happy about paying them.

Reporters besiege Frank's car outside Old Trafford after he had been sacked by Manchester United on December 19, 1972, just days after a 5-0 defeat at Crystal Palace.

They called me into the board meeting and around the table were all the directors. Matt sat on the far side. I kept my wits about me but the chairman said "we are terminating your contract." Everyone was silent and Matt had his head down, so I asked for a reason, which kind of took them all aback. We weren't bottom of the table so I asked why I was being sacked.

I wanted a reason and Louis said there was no reason. I said I'm not leaving until I get one as I'd look stupid being sacked if I didn't know the reason.

The chairman said that we were bottom of the table, but in fact we were third from bottom, while Matt never said a word, just kept his head down.

Louis was quoted in the press that they would honour my contract so I assumed that would be the case. I wasn't shocked when it wasn't paid up as I knew the kind of people they were. David Meek, a journalist on the Manchester Evening News, had publicly backed me sometime before and as a result the board banned him from travelling to away games on the team coach.

I was 18 months into my contract and I sought legal advice. I went to the Professional Footballers' Association and Cliff Lloyd gave me the name of George Davis, their solicitor, and I went and had a talk with a Mr Tongue. He told me my rights, what I had to do and that we should sue them for wrongful dismissal. I was a bit anxious about suing Manchester United - I was doubtful that if the case was to be settled in court, I might not get a fair trial.

Then they stopped my salary, even though Malcolm Musgrove had been fully paid up. I was advised by Mr Tongue to see the QC Mr Ben Hytner, who would represent me if the case went to court, and I said "Look tell me if I'm out of order, but I've got a niggle and I have to say it. I'm suing Manchester United but I've seen some of the circuit court judges at Old Trafford and if I get one of them I may not get a fair deal."

He said "Don't worry Frank - for a start, I'm a Manchester City supporter!" I told him that was good news and he had reassured me. He said not to worry, he would get Matt Busby in the witness box but it was going to take time to prepare everything. In the end it took nine months for the case to come to court, during which I had no money.

The night I got sacked Brian Clough rang my house. Ann took

all the calls and Cloughie said he was sorry to hear about Frank, telling her "they're a shower of bastards. But never mind, have a Happy Christmas."

The following day he sent three bouquets of flowers - one for Ann and one for each of my daughters. Cloughie could come across as bombastic on television while Matt Busby always came across as nice and my youngest daughter said "Isn't it funny how the good people sometimes turn out to be bad and the bad people turn out to be good."

Why John Aston and Jimmy Murphy got the sack at the same time as me, I will never fathom out. John had been at Old Trafford all his life, and his son, John junior, had played for United in the 1968 European Cup final at Wembley. I think when I started bringing new players in John thought it was about time - nothing had been done for years. He'd made recommendations that hadn't been followed up and he fully supported me, which is probably why he was dismissed.

Jimmy Murphy was a very good scout and had been a brick for United after the Munich air disaster. But he was treated very shabbily. He always had the club at heart but at the end they argued over his pension and took his taxi away from him - he didn't drive and used to take a cab from his house to the ground. Jimmy and his family were very bitter about how it all ended.

Tommy Docherty came in after me and eventually got rid of players and United were relegated the following season. I think there was probably a line of thought to get rid of anyone I had brought in.

They stayed up the season I was sacked, then the Doc had a full season in charge and they went down - and he didn't get the sack! I got sacked supposedly because United were at the bottom of the table, and yet the Doc didn't, even though they were relegated.

In fact when Matt Busby became manager of Manchester United in 1945 and inherited players like Johnny Carey, John Aston, Jack Rowley and Henry Cockburn, it took him three years to win his first trophy, the FA Cup in 1948, and he didn't win his first League title until 1951 - so there was no instant success there.

I had to sign on the dole after being sacked and I asked to see the manager of the Salford Labour Exchange on the quiet. I was conscious the children were at school and I had to pay their fees and I didn't want them to be hurt by the publicity of me being sacked. I had never signed on the dole in my life as I had always worked since leaving school. I was concerned that one of the tabloid newspapers would take a photo of me going into the Labour Exchange. I didn't want that for my family, so the manager let me go in the back way. I took Ann in for support and you could relate to the people who hadn't got a job. I remember seeing men outside the Labour Exchange in Cork many years before who couldn't find work, and I could now empathise with them.

I was out of work until the following October when the case was due to come to court. We managed the best we could, but we ran up a little bit of debt here and there. There was a time when my daughters' friends even stopped ringing. Not out of malice, but embarrassment.

The night I got sacked, two of Matt Busby's friends, Canon Lakin, who was a parish priest in Manchester, and a bookmaker called Johnny Foy, came around to express their regret. They felt it was wrong. Johnny, God rest his soul, said "I don't know how

Frank kept himself fit by running in the local park after having his contract terminated by Manchester United.

you're fixed, and don't know when you'll get any money, but you can have £10,000 from me anytime you want and pay me back whenever you can." I never took the money but thanked him all the same. It was a very generous gesture, especially as he and Canon Lakin had been friends of Matt for many years.

Someone else who had been close to Matt, Frank Ford, who was managing director of a coach company in Blackpool, rang and asked if he could take me out to lunch. I had never met him, but I knew he loaned his Rolls Royce to the German surgeon who had operated on Matt in Munich every time he came to England to see Matt. He told me he didn't agree with what had happened and he invited Ann and me for a fortnight's cruise on his hired yacht around the Greek islands.

It was a very kind offer and initially I was reluctant to accept, but Ann said it might be rude to turn it down. He paid our flights

Frank used some of his spare time after being sacked by Manchester United by accompanying some handicapped children on a pilgrimage to Lourdes in France.

over to Cyprus and while we were over there I met Wilf McGuinness, who had also been sacked by Manchester United in 1970 after 18 months in charge, having also taken over from Matt Busby.

On the flight back from Greece, we stopped off in Rome and went to a Papal Audience at The Vatican, and also visited the Sistine Chapel.

Among other good people who showed their loyalty and kindness were members of the Irish Society, Chris Rocke, Tommy Fallon and Tony Deacy, who took me to play golf, along with the hundreds of fans who wrote letters in response to my sacking.

I was also a good friend of Denis Lowe, the BBC Grandstand reporter who wrote for the Daily Telegraph, and he'd ask me to go to games with him to get me out of the house. That was very helpful.

In 1973 when I had plenty of free time, I took the opportunity to go to Lourdes with some children, as part of a trip organised by the Handicapped Children's Pilgrimage Trust. I went as a helper with the Liverpool group. I rang them up, paid my own fare and it took me away from the mayhem for a while. I said a few prayers and thanked my lucky stars.

I pushed a wheelchair for two twin boys who had something wrong with their lungs. I sat up with them at nights as you had to turn them over a few times because of the fluid build-up. It was a very rewarding week and losing my job was nothing compared with what those children had to cope with. It helped me keep the whole business in perspective.

What had happened was no big deal. I'd lost my job but my wife and girls were OK. But I got hurt by it.

It wasn't so much that I got the sack but the way they behaved as people. I can never forgive them for that - they were nasty beggars.

EVENTS OF 1974

Famine caused by drought threatened millions in Africa.

USA president Richard Nixon resigned in the Watergate scandal.

The IRA began a bombing campaign in mainland Britain.

A wind speed of 125 mph was recorded in Kilkeel, Co. Down.

The energy crisis meant Football League games were played on midweek afternoons.

Frank O'Farrell accepted the post of manager of Iran.

6

OUR MAN IN TEHRAN

*I believe for every drop of rain that falls
a flower grows,
I believe that somewhere in the darkest night
a candle glows,
I believe for everyone who goes astray,
Someone will come to show the way ...*

The Bachelors (Drake, Graham, Shirl & Stillman)

I DID a spot of gardening and took Ann out shopping - I'd never really had time for that before. Denis Lowe continued taking me to a few matches and I agreed to do a bit of scouting for West Ham. A lot of people rang up and sympathised and wanted to help but I had to wait for the court case before I could get another job.

Then just before the case was due to come up, Manchester United settled my claim. They obviously didn't want to go to court and I don't think Matt would have relished facing Mr Hytner in the witness box. I got a call from my solicitor and he had the cheque but they had forgotten to deduct the tax so I got the full amount. The club had to pay the tax when it was due as I had gone to Iran by then. The settlement was about £45,000 - and they had to pay the legal costs as well. I'd gone almost a year without any money so I felt justice had been done.

Soon after the settlement, I had a call out of the blue from Cardiff City. They were struggling at the bottom of Division Two and their chairman, David Goldstone, asked whether I would go down and help out, and see what could be done. I went and though I didn't sign a contract - I had asked for three years - he said if I could keep them in Division Two he'd give me £1,000 as a bonus.

Jimmy Andrews was out of work so I took him with me as

coach. Malcolm Musgrove had by then gone to Bournemouth with John Bond. Malcolm has since passed away but happily we still keep in close touch with his wife Jean, who lives in Torquay.

The family stayed up north and I was in a hotel in Cardiff near the rugby ground, and I often used to chat with the Welsh rugby players who stayed there before a match. I went home most weekends. I was there just for the rest of the season and though we got some reasonable results, it was touch and go whether we would stay up.

I took Willie Carlin, who I had signed at Leicester, on loan from Notts County and also signed John Farrington from Leicester for £62,000, and later in the season I signed goalkeeper Ron Healey from Manchester City and Clive Charles from West Ham.

Malcolm Allison was manager of Crystal Palace and Palace came to Ninian Park for the last match, a game Cardiff had to draw to stay up. We got the result we needed, a 1-1 draw, and Palace went down instead. It had been hard, but in the end I had helped Cardiff maintain their Division Two status, which is what I set out to achieve when I went there.

Ann and Frank can still enjoy a joke as they tend to their garden in Manchester after Frank had left United.

I wasn't actually in charge for that last game, even though I was there at Ninian Park, as I had by then agreed a two-year contract to manage the Iranian national side.

I had received a phone call out of the blue from a Mr Shariat, who was representing the Iranian Football Association. He had followed events in England, had seen I'd been sacked at Manchester United and wondered if I would be interested in going to Iran to manage the national team.

Iran was staging the Asian Games in Tehran in September, 1974 and they really wanted to put on a good show. He said they had great weightlifters and boxers and the like, but football attracted the most people and they wanted a good football team too. He asked whether I would meet him in London, which I did, and I accepted their offer of a two-year contract in April 1974.

During my time in Wales, I also got a phone call on New Year's Day after a game at Portsmouth to say my mother, who was 75, had died. She had suffered a brain haemorrhage on her way to Mass and died in the street. In Ireland they bury people very quickly, two nights in the church and then they are buried, so I had to make some hasty arrangements to get to the funeral. It was very similar to when my dad had died in 1962 while I was at Weymouth. He'd had a gall bladder removed and never recovered, even though it should have been a straightforward operation. He was 67.

When my mother died, my bookmaker friend, Johnny Foy, helped organise a flight from Manchester to Dublin. Then I got the train from Dublin to Cork and I just made it to the funeral.

The Cardiff chairman didn't want me to go to Iran but I said he couldn't stop me because I didn't have a contract. He then said that therefore he didn't owe me £1,000 either! I could have stayed at Cardiff, but to be honest I wanted to get away from the cauldron of English football after what I'd been through. I wanted to clear my mind and look at things from a different perspective.

The Manchester United experience had left a nasty taste and made me think a lot. They were supposed to be the good guys setting an example, but they weren't and they didn't set an example in the way they treated me. The most powerful should act in a proper way so they can be a model for others to follow - not like our MPs in Parliament who in recent times failed to distinguish between what were legitimate expenses and stealing!

It was an enormous task going to a strange country but I needed to get away and Iran appealed to me. Brian Clough had been offered the job but he went out there and turned it down. I rang him up to find out why and he just said "it's not for me Frank, but I wouldn't recommend anyone turning it down". He'd made some disparaging remarks about not seeing many Rolls Royces over there, but that was typical Cloughie!

The Iranians are a great people with wonderful traditions, and a very intelligent nation. They'd built this big new stadium that could hold 120,000 people and the success of the games hinged on the success of the football side. They were good at other sports but football was the number one sport and they wanted to win the gold medal.

Frank signs on the dotted line as manager of Iran, watched by fellow English coach George Skinner. The big picture on the wall behind them is of the Shah of Iran.

Iran is a large country, and the capital, Tehran, had a population of four million in 1974. It was a large metropolis and in the south of the city you could watch craftsmen and women at work creating beautiful Persian carpets stitch by stitch. Dominating the city was Mount Damavand, the highest peak in the country at 18,000 feet, part of the Alborz range of mountains that would be covered in snow until the last white spot disappeared in June each year.

The north of the country was as green as the British Isles with very fertile land to grow fruit, vegetables and wheat. Caviar was harvested in the Caspian Sea, which separates Iran from Russia, and one of my assistant coaches used to bring me some when he joined us in Tehran in preparation for games.

Iran, while being a modern nation, is also the repository of ancient civilisation and cultures going back to the Achaemenian dynasty 500 years BC.

The most important Achaemenian monument is found in Persepolis near the city of Shiraz. Persepolis is a complex of palaces by Darius and completed by his son Xerxes. It is recorded in the Bible how Cyrus the Persian had freed the Jews from captivity in Babylon. The ruins of these palaces are something to behold. Shiraz is known as the city of roses, and the home of the poets Hafiz and Sadi, and is a really beautiful place. Isfahan is the ancient capital of Persia, a city of beautiful mosques, palaces and bridges, and with some lovely parks. Down in the south of the country it was more barren and very hot where the oil wells were near Abadan.

When I first went over to Iran, I was met at the airport, signed into the hotel, and then all the lights went out! I thought this is a good omen, in the dark in a strange hotel. Fortunately someone lit a candle so I could walk up the stairs.

Ann and I settled in well in our home and there were no problems. Bernadette was at teacher training college so she stayed in England, but Catherine went to an English college in Iran. Ann would meet other English and American people when she visited the supermarket nearby and we made two very good American friends in Graham and Helen Hancock, who later came to see us in England on their way back to the USA.

We then visited them in Seattle the following year and they

took us in their car down through Oregon and California, through the Redwood Forest and driving through that massive redwood tree, on our way to San Francisco, where we did a tour of Alcatraz Prison. It was a lovely holiday in the company of lovely people. Sadly they are dead now but it was a real joy to have known them.

In Tehran we could listen to BBC radio and there was also a US Army radio station that broadcast good music. We could get the English papers and we went to some shows. We actually saw Norman Wisdom while we were over there and his performance was well received. We got invited to dinners and alcohol was usually available if you wanted it.

I was given a translator named Kiumars Soroushiari for the duration of my stay and remarkably he had been a student at Leicester University while I was manager of Leicester and was a fan. It was a big joy for him for me to come out and manage Iran, and we got on really well. A lot of the Iranian players were students who spoke English and I used to help them with their English grammar. I also picked up some of their language, Farsi.

The standard of the players was probably like Division Three in England at the time. They had good skills and good physique, they trained well and always wanted to learn. Some of the things they could do would have people out of their seats. They were mainly brought up on stony pitches so they had good ball control.

There were also a couple of English coaches out there as the FA had a policy of sending coaches abroad to help develop the game. They were George Skinner, who had played for Tottenham, and Alan Rogers, who was with Persepolis, one of the top clubs. They were both very helpful to me as they had a good knowledge of the Iranian players.

I also met the Shah and Empress Farah at the Asian games, which went really well for us. We beat Pakistan, Burma, who were coached by Bert Trautmann, and I was delighted to meet him, Bahrain, Malaysia, South Korea and Iraq to reach the final against Israel. We only conceded one goal in those six qualifying games, and scored 19.

There wasn't the animosity between Iran and Israel as there is now, and the final was a 120,000 sell-out. My assistant coach, Heshmat Moharjerani, who was a policeman from Mechei on the Russian border, asked me if I could get him a few more seat tickets for the final for some friends. I could only get standing tickets but Heshmat was not happy and didn't want to take them. I put it to him like this "Heshmat you have a choice. If your friends want to see the game badly enough they can have the standing tickets. If you refuse the tickets, the alternative is that they stand outside the

Frank on the rostrum with some of the Iranian team who won the football tournament at the 1974 Asian Games. In the foreground is Crown Prince Reza (left), who Frank coached during his time in Iran, and his uncle, Prince Gholam Reza.

The Iranian squad who emerged victorious at the 1974 Asian Games in Tehran. Frank is on the extreme right of the front row.

IRAN in 1974 ASIAN GAMES

QUALIFYING GROUP D

September 3	Pakistan	7-0
September 5	Burma	2-1
September 7	Bahrain	6-0

seventh asian games

TEHRAN 1974

Table	P	W	D	L	F	A	Pts
Iran	3	3	0	0	15	1	6
Burma	3	2	0	1	10	3	4
Pakistan	3	1	0	2	6	13	2
Bahrain	3	0	0	3	1	15	0

SEMI-FINALS, GROUP A

September 9	Malaysia	1-0
September 11	South Korea	2-0
September 13	Iraq	1-0

Table	P	W	D	L	F	A	Pts
Iran	3	3	0	0	4	0	6
Malaysia	3	1	1	1	3	3	3
Iraq	3	0	2	1	1	2	2
South Korea	3	0	1	2	3	6	1

FINAL (September 15. Attendance: 120,000) **IRAN 1** (Itzhak Shum, 30 og) **ISRAEL 0**
Iran: Nasser Hejazi, Masih Masih-Nia, Akbar Kargharjam, Jaafar Kashani, Izzat Janmalaki, Ali Jabbari, Ali Parvin, Parviz Ghleechkhani, Mohamad Sadeghi, Golam Hussain Mazloomi, Mohamad Reza Adelkhani (Hasan Rowshan 66).
Israel: Itzik Visoker, Avraham Lev, Zvi Rozen, Yeshaayahu Schwager, Menahem Bello, Meir Nimni, Itzhak Shum, Moshe Schweitzer, Gidi Damti (Moshe Onana 46), Yehoshua Feigenbaum (Yoel Massuari 68), Shalom Schwartz.
Referee: Mohammed Azam (India).

Frank's record as manager of Iran was 10 wins, two draws and three defeats in 15 games.

stadium looking at a blank wall and see nothing. That is the choice, and it is the only choice available to you." He took the tickets and agreed with me that bad tickets were better than no tickets.

One ceremony which I didn't find very pleasant, to say the least, was when the team were leaving the training camp to go to the stadium for the final a sheep had been slaughtered and the players walked through the blood to get to the coach. It was a traditional custom.

We won the final 1-0 and I felt like I had achieved something. After what had happened at United, it was a great boost and we became celebrities in the country. It was also a fillip for Iran as it was the first time a Middle Eastern country had won the football event at the Asian Games. They also ended up qualifying for the World Cup finals in 1978, and that was basically with my team.

The Shah thanked me for what I had done and asked for guidance on the future. I said they should play better teams, because even if you lose, you learn.

Empress Farah asked if I would visit the palace once a week to take her son, Crown Prince Reza, who was about 15 years old, for football practice with his classmates. I did this for some time and it was a good experience. I asked how I should address the young Prince and was told if I was talking to him in a formal manner, I should call him Your Highness, but in class I could call him Reza.

The Prince was a left-winger and quite a useful player but

The English papers kept track of Frank while he was managing Iran. Part of the article on the right reads: 'After last night's triumph (the 1-0 victory over Israel in the football final at the 1974 Asian Games) he has become almost as big a national figure as the Shah of Iran.'

Frank O'Farrell is hero of Iran

FRANK O'FARRELL, the football manager who turned his back on Britain, was today the hero of Iran.

For last night, in front of 100,000 fans at the Aryamehr Stadium, Teheran, the Iran national team, which O'Farrell manages, beat Israel 1-0 to win the Asian Games football title.

As the Iranian players stepped up on to the gold medal rostrum, they called on O'Farrell to join them, and the crowd were soon chanting his name.

The quietly-spoken O'Farrell seemed overcome by it all, but he was reassured by the presence of his wife and two children, who joined in the applause for the man who has been manager of the team for only five months.

Bitter man

O'Farrell took over the Iranian team in May on a two-year contract, reputed to be worth £40,000 plus fringe benefits. He has become almost as big a national figure as the Shah of Iran.

O'Farrell was formerly manager of Leicester City, Manchester United and Cardiff City. His sacking by Manchester United left him a bitter man, but now he says: "That is all in the past. It never pays to look back."

He still takes a keen interest in British football, and gives the impression that one day he will come back home. But for the time being he is fully involved in Iran's emergence on the football scene.

"I like the set-up here, the people and the facilities," he says. "Our present team is getting a bit old, and I plan to bring some younger players together for a tournament in Vietnam in October."

World Cup bid

"Then we have got to start thinking about the Olympics and the 1978 World Cup." Iran only narrowly missed qualifying for Asia's representatives in the 1970 World Cup finals, losing to Australia 3-2 on aggregate.

But whether O'Farrell will spend the rest of his football career in Iran is open to question. He regularly scans the papers for the English League results, and is keenly interested in the recent managerial shake-ups back home.

"But at the moment, I'm glad to be here," he says. "Tell the people back in Britain that I can manage teams to win."

FRANK O'FARRELL — still interested in British soccer.

O'Farrell plans to spend the next few days quietly with his family, but it will be difficult to avoid the back-slapping and hand-shakes which will accompany him wherever he goes.

Soccer is the number one sport in Iran—as shown by the fact that during the 15 days of the Asian games the Aryamehr Stadium was only ever full when Iran were playing football there.

sometimes, like most youngsters, he would mess about while I was trying to make a point. So I gave him ten press-ups to do and the other lads looked on in amazement that some foreign layman could make the next ruler of Iran do press-ups!

Fair play to him, he did them and then got on with the exercises we'd be doing. I hope that experience might have helped him later following the revolution that forced his family to leave Iran and make the adjustment to living in a normal environment like the rest of us. He was a very nice boy and I was sorry when I witnessed how his family were treated, when only Mr Sadat of Egypt would give the Shah refuge. I wrote to Colonel Sadat thanking him for his kind gesture and I received a nice reply from him. Sadat was later assassinated by a gunman in his own country.

During our stay in Iran, there was no difficulty getting to Mass as there were a number of churches in Tehran, and Mass centres in other cities. The only difference was that Friday was the Muslim Holy Day and the equivalent of our Sunday, which was an ordinary working day there. So the church adapted to the custom and Christians went to their services on Fridays. The Armenians were the largest Christian group in Iran, and a few of them were Catholic.

There was a strange coincidence when I met the only other O'Farrell in Iran at the time. I went into the bank one day and noticed a sum of money had been lodged in my account and had been sent from Ireland. I knew it was not for me and discovered it should have been lodged in the account of a Reverend Father O'Farrell, a young Irish Dominican priest, and had been sent to him by his mother in Dublin. He was down in Shiraz at the time and I went to see him, to tell him what had happened and to give him his money.

I stayed in Iran a couple of years and during that time the youth team went to the Asian Youth Games in Kuwait and the senior team qualified for the Montreal Olympics in 1976. One of the Iranian youth team who I took to Kuwait was an Armenian Christian named Baghdig Abedian. While we were there he presented me with a beautiful gold cross and chain. I was very touched by the gesture and I still wear it to this day.

The Sheikh of Kuwait also gave me a lovely wrist watch and many years later I was filling up my car with petrol in the UK and the chap behind the counter said what a nice watch it was. He was a bit taken aback when I said the Sheikh of Kuwait had given it to me!

My coach, Heshmat, took over from me when I left Iran before the 1976 Olympics, but I had done what I set out to do and I was happy. They had appreciated me being there and treated me very well. They gave me a nice going away party and a splendid Persian rug. It all ended very friendly, a far better experience than how it had ended in Manchester.

One of my friends had warned me before I went to Iran "Be careful Frank, they're a funny lot over there." I said I had just come from a funny lot up at Old Trafford. They surely couldn't be much funnier than that!

I returned briefly to Iran in 1978, ahead of the World Cup in Argentina, with a BBC team including John Motson. They were doing a feature on the Iranian team and they used me to help with the introductions, and as a guide. Iran drew 1-1 with Scotland in the 1978 World Cup finals but lost to both Holland (3-0) and Peru (4-1).

More recently, in 2006, I was invited back to Iran, along with Alan Rogers. All the air fares were paid and we were put up in a top hotel. I met the players from the 1974 team again. I have a soft

Frank (right) and Alan Rogers, who coached Persepolis, were both invited back to Iran in 2006 and feted as heroes. Rogers, the uncle of former Tranmere Rovers chairwoman Lorraine Rogers, coached in numerous countries during a nomadic career, including the Philippines, Africa, America, Qatar, Cyprus and Iceland, as well as a enjoying couple of spells in Iran.

spot for Iran even now, despite what has happened over there.

Revolutions are brutal and some of the generals who I got to know were killed. I saw a photograph of 13 generals laid out naked on the floor, having been executed by the revolutionary forces. I don't know what their crimes were, but no-one deserved a fate like that. I knew one or two of them through football and the whole thing shocked me deeply.

When Ann and I returned from Iran to our home in Manchester in 1976, I got a call from Tony Boyce at Torquay asking if I would go back there as manager as they had dismissed Malcolm Musgrove. I told him I didn't wish to manage in the Fourth Division again as it was something I had already done. He then asked me to go back as general manager if they appointed a player-manager or player-coach. He felt with my contacts, I might be able to recruit players who could be improved and then sold on to bring much-needed cash into the club. I agreed to have a go on that basis.

Frank enjoys a joke on his return to Iran with the BBC team in 1978. Pictured on the left is John Motson.

Within a few weeks, Newcastle United wanted me as their manager. I went for an interview, driving to Newcastle and back to Torquay in a day, and they offered me a five-year contract at £25,000 a year, a very generous offer.

But this time I put Ann first and decided it wouldn't be fair for her to move again, having just got settled in Torquay. It was a choice between a quiet civilised life or the call of the wild, but I never felt football should dominate your life to the point where its values are the only ones you have. The job eventually went to Bill McGarry.

I was caretaker-manager at Torquay for a few months until they appointed Mike Green as player-manager, and I became general manager. Then the club recruited Bruce Rioch as player-coach to succeed Mike Green in 1981 and I took on the role of manager again, and then general manager. Bruce was appointed manager in July 1982 and I stayed on as general manager until the end of the 1982-83 season, when I finally retired.

During that second spell at Torquay, we had some success in bringing in players, and selling them on. One of them was Colin Lee, a Devon-born striker who I signed from Bristol City in January 1977, and who scored on his debut.

He netted 10 goals in 23 games before a £60,000 move to Tottenham Hotspur less than a year after joining us. He famously scored four goals on his Tottenham debut in a 9-0 demolition of Bristol Rovers that was shown on Match of the Day. Colin has returned to Plainmoor in recent years, first as caretaker manager, then director of football and chief executive, but he has since left the club.

Bruce Rioch came in when the club were struggling financially and his first board meeting was a real eye opener for him. We had signed Tony 'Bomber' Brown, who had enjoyed an illustrious career with West Bromwich Albion. He took a while to settle in and at this particular board meeting, one of the directors named Mark Spedding, started ranting about Tony Brown being useless. I tried to explain how he was trying to adjust to Fourth Division football - he was making runs like he did in the First Division, but he wasn't getting the same quality of service.

This director didn't want to listen to my explanations so I said to the chairman, Tony Boyce, that I obviously can't satisfy Mr

Spedding, he is not prepared to listen to me, so please excuse me I'm leaving. I got up, excused myself and left the room.

I stayed on at the club until the end of the season and then I retired. Bruce tells me he gets great satisfaction from relating that story to people wherever he has coached.

Shortly after I retired Tony Boyce rang me and said there had been a fight at the club involving Bruce and a player, Colin Anderson. I rang Bruce and he said it was down to frustration. I told him not to resign, make them sack you if they want. But in the end he did resign, though he went on to have a good managerial career at Middlesbrough, Bolton Wanderers, Arsenal, Norwich City, Millwall and Wigan Athletic, and he had some success in Denmark as well.

During my last spell at Torquay, I was invited to manage the Al-Shaab club in Sharjah, in the United Arab Emirates. I went out there but only stayed about six months as the young Sheikh Faisal did not fulfil his promises in providing a house, and Ann and I had to live in a hotel. One night we went to dinner in the hotel

Welcome home. Frank returned to Torquay United in 1976 when he returned from Iran. Also pictured are players (left to right) Dave Stocks, Dave Kennedy, Clint Boulton and Ian Twitchin.

and the head waiter said he could not give us dinner because Sheikh Faisal had not paid the bill. When I told Sheikh Faisal the story, he just moved us to another hotel, but it was not a good environment in which to work so I packed it in and we returned to live in Torquay, where we are still living now. Don Revie was in the Emirates at the time but he was with one of the best clubs, and I met up with him while I was out there.

Football has changed so much in so many ways in the last 50 years, most notably in the remuneration of the players compared to the old days. I'd like to be playing now and earning the money they earn, though I can't really get my head around some of the figures. Manchester United are allegedly £300 million in debt - how does that work? The TV companies also seem to have the upper hand these days, deciding when matches are to be played, all for their own benefit.

I really do fear for the future of the game at times. The banks have had their problems and I can see more clubs getting into difficulty for trying to over-achieve.

I still look out for the scores and I am always made very welcome down at Torquay United, where I have a seat in the directors' box. I even went to Old Trafford at the end of last season (May, 2011) when Torquay qualified for the League Two play-off final against Stevenage Borough.

It was the first time I had been back to the ground since I was sacked by United in 1972, and though Torquay lost 1-0, it was good to be able go back there after so long.

Subsequently I have been back to Old Trafford again, and to The Cliff, the club's training ground, to be interviewed for an Irish TV documentary. I have to say that I received a very warm welcome from everyone I met there, including Wilf McGuinness.

I also look out for the Preston, West Ham and Leicester scores. I still have some emotion for those clubs, and I was saddened to see West Ham and Preston both relegated last season. I have a real affinity for those two clubs and I really enjoyed playing for them.

At Preston, there is an excellent Former Players' Association and we meet up for a few events each year. Ian and Eric Rigby do a fantastic job in keeping it going. We always have a great night at the annual dinner - there is always lots to talk and reminisce about. Some of the team I played with have now passed on, Les

Frank (left) serving Mass with Bill Derry at Our Lady Help of Christians and St Denis, St Mary church in Torquay. The celebrant is Father George Carrick.

Frank, in the middle of the picture in the flat cap, during the Paris to Chartres three-day, 70-mile Catholic pilgrimage.

Dagger very recently, and sadly Tom Finney is not so well these days. But Tommy Thompson, Sammy Taylor, Fred Else and Derek Mayers are usually there each year and it is a real joy for me to see them.

When I finally left Torquay United, I had some free time and my parish priest asked me if I would start up a branch of the St Vincent de Paul Society in the parish. It is a worldwide Catholic organisation formed in the 19th Century in Paris by a group of young university students led by Frederick Ozanam. Their main work is helping the poor, visiting the sick and other charitable work.

I also started serving daily Mass for the late Father Foley, who was one of the few priests who continued to celebrate the old Latin Mass after the New Order of Mass in English was introduced in 1969. After he died I served daily Mass in the parish until recently, when I had to give up owing to my knee problems giving me trouble and making it difficult to kneel down. At 83 I must have been one of the oldest servers.

I was tidying up one day after serving at a Requiem Mass, taking the sacred vessels into the Sacristy, when a man who was at the Mass approached, having obviously recognised me. He said "I wonder if Fergie (Sir Alex Ferguson) will do this when he retires." We had a good laugh about that.

Between my mid-60s and mid-70s, I walked eight times in the famous Chartres Pilgrimage. This is a pilgrimage in which 10,000 Catholics walk from Notre Dame Cathedral in Paris to Chartres Cathedral, 70 miles south-east of Paris, over three days in all weathers, sleeping in tents at night. The Traditional Latin Mass, or the Extraordinary Rite which Pope Benedict termed it recently, is celebrated each day, culminating in a Solemn High Mass in Chartres Cathedral on the final day to bring the pilgrimage to a close.

I am feeling much more optimistic about the future of the Traditional Rite of Mass now. Pope Benedict, when he was Cardinal Ratzinger, stated that some of the problems in the church were due to the "disintegration of the liturgy." When he became Pope, he improved the situation when he published 'Summorum Pontificum' in 2007, where he stated the Old Rite of Mass "had never been abrogated" and priests could celebrate it without asking their bishop for permission.

He was obviously aware of many bishops making it difficult for those Catholics wanting the Old Mass to get it. So a priest can celebrate the Old Mass now if people request it, providing he is comfortable with it.

It is very encouraging to see more priests going on training courses to become competent at celebrating it, even if some of our bishops are not happy at seeing their power to prevent it taken away from them. Deo gratias. My prayers said on the long walks to Chartres are being answered.

I used to go on the pilgrimage feeling a bit discouraged, having experienced the unhelpfulness and even the hostility of our bishops and clergy to anyone who asked for a greater number of celebrations for the Traditional Latin Mass.

Then I started to walk in the Chartres pilgrimage and I discovered I was not walking with people of my own age group, but with young families, young Catholics and young priests all devoted to the Old Mass and I knew things were going to get better for us. Pope John Paul II tried to improve the situation for us in 1988 when in his Motu Proprio 'Ecclesia Dei' he said we had "legitimate aspirations". His plea was generally ignored by the bishops and I feel he should have used stronger language to the bishops than he did.

Pope Benedict, in his letter to the bishops, said "What earlier generations held as sacred remains sacred and great for us too, and it cannot be all of a sudden entirely forbidden or even harmful." Well said, your Holiness. Bishops please take note.

He also said in his letter that "immediately after the Second Vatican Council, it was presumed that requests for the use of the 1962 Missal would be limited to the older generation (like me) who had grown up with it, but in the meantime it has clearly been demonstrated that young people have also discovered this liturgical form, felt its attraction and found in it a form of encounter with the Mystery of the Most Holy Eucharist particularly suited to them."

Apart from the spiritual benefit of the walk to Chartres, I wrote begging letters to people to support the children's charities I was walking for. I had a good response from David Davies at the Football Association, from Gordon Taylor of the Professional

Frank lives in retirement on the Devon coast.

Former Leicester City player and club ambassador Alan Birchenall interviews Frank on a visit to Filbert Street.

Frank with his great grandson Callum Francis.

Footballers' Association, and from Bruce Rioch and others. The Children's Hospice, the School for the Deaf in Exeter and the Plymouth Children's Society were some of the charities that benefitted - and they were all very grateful.

Once again my connection with football had helped bring some good to the world. It's amazing how something as simple as a game of football can have such a huge impact on people's lives.

When I reflect on my personal journey, I think back to how I could have died three times yet somehow I survived to tell the tale. I'm 84 and I can honestly say I've enjoyed my life. I have a great wife, children and grandchildren, and a great grandson, Callum Francis, so what do I have to complain about?

I was an Irish choirboy who had a fulfilling football career, played in what is now known as the Premiership, represented my country, managed at international level, and was in charge of both an FA Cup final team and possibly the most famous club side in the world.

Would I change anything if I could go back and start all over again? You bet I would - but just the one thing.

I'd have loved to have driven that express train to Dublin!

TALKING OF FRANK

TONY DRUMMOND
(a team-mate of Frank's at Cork United in the late 1940s.
Tony's career was ended by injury in his early 20s. He is now 89)

EVEN as a teenager, Frank had a great touch and he was
always very cool and composed on the ball. You could see he
possessed a good football brain and he played an important
role at wing-half in linking the defence and the attack.

I remembered he worked on the railway like his father, and
he was a really good guy.

I think most folk in Cork followed his career after he left for
England and we were proud to see him go on and do so well. It
was a major talking point in the city when he was appointed
manager of Manchester United in 1971.

I met up with Frank again in recent years when he was
guest of honour at City Hall in Cork and he has not changed.
He is still that lovely, friendly lad who I played alongside for
Cork United in the 1946-47 season, when we won the Irish
Shield with a 1-0 win over Shelbourne in the final.

JOHN BOND
(a West Ham team-mate of Frank's who also played under him
at Torquay United. He went on to manage Bournemouth,
Norwich City and Manchester City)

THERE were quite a few Irishmen at West Ham at that time
like Danny McGowan and Noel Cantwell and Frank was as
good as any of them. He probably wasn't as skilful as the
others but his attitude was good and he carried that attitude
with him into management.

One incident really sticks out in my mind and it was when
we were playing against Tottenham. I was at right-back playing
against Cliff Jones who I never used to like playing against
because he was so quick and could really play. All of a sudden
somebody got injured at inside-right and so Cliff moved from

the left-wing to inside-right and Frank shouted over to me "John, you can come and play left-half now and I'll play right back." I shouted back at him "Actually Frank, you can p*** off." That's just a little memory I have of him.

When Frank went to Torquay as manager, he asked me to sign for the Devon club. I went down to see him and I told him I didn't want to move down there so he said I could live in London and play for him at weekends.

So I did that and, mainly because of Frank, I put my head down and gave it everything I had and I had three very good years at Torquay.

In fact those three years were probably as good as any during my time at West Ham.

I liked Frank as a manager but he didn't stand any messing about. Because I knew him so well I guess I used to take a few liberties here and there but, overall, he would not accept people who didn't do their stuff on a Saturday afternoon.

I remember once he gave me the rollocking of all rollockings when we played at Crewe after I'd been through the motions a little bit and he said to me "if that's the way you're going to play, then you better go back." Frank just wouldn't tolerate that kind of thing.

He was a tough guy and he didn't take any prisoners. Nor did he stand on ceremony with you at all. If something had to be said he'd say it. I liked that about him because you knew exactly where you stood.

He would have a laugh with you but you needed to go out and give it your all in every game. If you did that, you were all right with him.

If you didn't then he'd let you know in no uncertain terms that he was not prepared to tolerate it and if you carried on then you'd be on your bike.

When he joined Manchester United, I don't think the players liked how he handled them. I think it may have been the players who got him out. Frank would get at people about their attitude and their approach to the game.

I think he went to United at the wrong time because they had too many star players and there were too many players who thought they could play and couldn't.

TOMMY THOMPSON

(former England international who was leading scorer for Preston
with 34 goals when they finished second in Division One
in the 1957-58 season)

I REMEMBER Frank as a good, solid wing-half and he has
become one of my favourite footballing friends.

I don't see him that often, but he does his best to get up to
the Preston Former Players Association annual dinners and it is
always a great occasion to meet up with him again.

He is a lovely man and he is very popular with all the
former Preston players.

We had a really successful team at Preston in the late 1950s
and got so close to winning the title, finishing second and third
in the Division One table.

Frank played his full part in that success, and he
contributed a lot of the spade work for my 34 League goals in
the 1957-58 season.

He was a studious type of fellow and he was always very
level-headed. I suppose they were the right attributes to go on
and become a successful manager. It therefore came as no real
surprise when he did well at Weymouth, Torquay and Leicester
and got the job at Manchester United.

It is a pity things never worked out for him at Old Trafford,
but Frank still achieved an awful lot more than most in his
football career.

TOMMY SPRATT

(former Manchester United youngster who played under Frank
at both Weymouth and Torquay United)

FRANK signed me at Weymouth from Bradford Park Avenue,
but I only had one season there before joining him at Torquay
United. I remember my time at both Weymouth and Torquay as
being very enjoyable - and very successful too.

Frank was the best manager I played under during my
career. He was a disciplinarian, but he always liked to look after
people and treat them the right way. He was also very family-

orientated and I always got on with him well. I don't really recall any fall-outs, but I do remember one occasion when I stayed overnight in Newcastle (where I came from) after we had played at either Darlington or Hartlepool.

I got up at 5am on the Monday morning to travel back to Torquay but six inches of snow had fallen during the night and I was obviously struggling to get back.

I rang him from Nottingham to tell him I didn't think I would make it and he just said "Well I will see you at training in the morning then!"

JOHN FARRINGTON
(a flying winger who Frank signed twice, first at Leicester City in 1969 and then at Cardiff City in 1973)

FRANK is a lovely, genuine person and both he and Malcolm Musgrove were great people to work for.

Leicester were a really friendly club and it helped me that Malcolm came from the same village as me, Lynemouth in Northumberland. I felt at home as soon as I joined them from Wolverhampton Wanderers in 1969.

I hadn't done myself justice at Wolves but my spell at Leicester were the best years of my career. It gave me the chance of regular first-team football and the 1970-71 Division Two title season was especially memorable.

Frank played football the way I liked it to be played. Both Frank and Malcolm worked with me to improve my game and they brought the best out of me. They encouraged me to get wide and get crosses in and that was my strength.

I also scored a few goals, and I was sad when Frank and Malcolm left to go to Manchester United in 1971.

Jimmy Bloomfield replaced him and started bringing in his own players, and I found myself sitting on the substitute's bench for a lot of the time.

When Frank took over at Cardiff City in 1973, I jumped at the chance to join up with him again, but things didn't work out, and I was disappointed when he left before the end of the season after getting the job in Iran.

I didn't stay long either before leaving for Northampton Town. But I have only fond memories of playing under Frank and Malcolm.

MARTIN BUCHAN

(cultured Manchester United and Scotland defender who Frank bought from Aberdeen during his time at Old Trafford)

WHEN I was at Aberdeen, I was told Manchester United, Liverpool and Leeds United were all monitoring my progress.

I had been impressed with what I had seen of Frank on TV, and he always came across as being very honest and an honourable man.

I met up with Frank, Matt Busby and John Aston at Bellshill and I knew Manchester United were looking for a replacement for David Sadler.

I made a telephone call to my former manager, Eddie Turnbull, who had been instrumental in my football education, and he said go for it. He said that while I might win more medals at Liverpool and Leeds, they might be Central League medals!

Teams were starting to get more organised in the early 1970s, and I think Frank and his assistant, Malcolm Musgrove, were keen to give more emphasis to organising the team. It was OK having flair, but organised teams would combat that and you needed good coaching.

The days of a manager saying "go out and enjoy yourselves" were coming to an end, but Frank had inherited an ageing squad and I think there was resistance to his ideas and methods.

At the end of the day, it is always about results and I suppose the results weren't good enough when it mattered.

Making such a good start in his first season, when United were clear at the top of the table at one stage, probably made things worse for him.

But I felt Frank was up against it from the start and I always retained a lot of respect for him.

TED MacDOUGALL

(prolific lower-division goalscorer who Frank took to Manchester
United from Third Division Bournemouth in 1972 for £200,000)

I WAS one of Frank's last signings at Old Trafford along with
Wyn Davies. Manchester United were still Manchester United,
but they were struggling at the time.

I particularly remember Frank's last game in charge at
Crystal Palace where we got beat 5-0 and Don Rogers scored
twice.

I came in at a particularly difficult time because there was
a turnaround of players. The Matt Busby era had ended, but he
was still upstairs, and there were a number of players who were
coming to the end of their careers.

There was a new regime and it wasn't going too well. We
had two different factions in the dressing room and we were
struggling. It was a very difficult situation for everyone, and
especially for Frank.

George Best was going AWOL. He was missing and we
never saw him. All that did was create an atmosphere that
wasn't conducive to a good dressing room or a good situation
on the pitch.

But Manchester United being Manchester United, you
were still getting 40, 50, 60,000 crowds, and you were still in a
goldfish bowl. It was a difficult job to get to grips with and you
were constantly under the spotlight.

Frank had gone from Leicester City to Manchester United,
and I know he had served his time at Weymouth and Torquay
United as well, but I don't think any experience in football
would make you comfortable at Manchester United unless you
had the freedom to do what you wanted and needed to do. I
don't think Frank had that.

I could see the writing on the wall, and I'm sure Frank
could too.

I felt sorry for him. Of course I did because Frank had taken
me to Old Trafford. He was the one who gave me the chance to
play for Manchester United.

FRANK'S PLAYING CAREER

POSITION: HALF-BACK

Season	Club	Division (Pos)	League A	League G	FA Cup A	FA Cup G
1950-51	West Ham United	2 (13th)	18	-	2	-
1951-52	West Ham United	2 (12th)	41	2	3	1
1952-53	West Ham United	2 (14th)	41	1	1	-
1953-54	West Ham United	2 (13th)	22	-	-	-
1954-55	West Ham United	2 (8th)	28	1	1	-
1955-56	West Ham United	2 (16th)	40	1	6	-
1956-57	West Ham United	2 (8th)	7	1	-	-
	Preston North End	1 (3rd)	18	1	6	1
1957-58	Preston North End	1 (2nd)	40	-	1	-
1958-59	Preston North End	1 (12th)	33	-	3	1
1959-60	Preston North End	1 (9th)	10	1	-	-
1960-61	Preston North End	1 (22nd)	17	-	1	-
			315	**8**		

		Southern A	Southern G	SL Cup A	SL Cup G	FA Cup A	FA Cup G
1961-62	Weymouth SL (6th)	31	4	5	-	4	-
1962-63	Weymouth SL (3rd)	40	5	6	2	2	-
1963-64	Weymouth SL (7th)	13	2	1	-	3	-
		84	**11**	**12**	**2**	**33**	**3**

Frank made 210 League and FA Cup appearances for West Ham scoring seven goals. He made 129 League and FA Cup appearances for Preston, netting four goals.

In all games, Frank made 117 appearances for Weymouth in all competitions, scoring 14 goals.

Frank also played for Clapton Celtic, Western Rovers & Cork United in Ireland.

FRANK'S INTERNATIONAL CAREER

REPUBLIC OF IRELAND - 9 caps (*denotes Frank scored)

May 7, 1952   Friendly v Austria (Vienna)   Lost 0-6   80,000

Austria: Musil, Rock, Happel, Hanappi, Ocwirk, Koller, Melchior, Decker, Dienst, Huber, Haummer.
Ireland: Kiernan, Martin, Fallon, Gannon, Aherne, O'Farrell, Eglington, Ringstead, Farrell, Fitzsimons, Ryan.
Goals: Huber 3, Dienst 2, Haummer.

March 25, 1953   Friendly v Austria (Dublin)   Won 4-0*   40,000

Ireland: O'Neill, Dunne, Lawler, Ringstead, Eglington, O'Farrell, Fitzsimons, Carey, Walsh, Farrell, Ryan.
Austria: Schweda, Stotz, Kowanz, Hanappi, Ocwirk, Koller, Kominek, Wagner, Huber, Stojaspal, Zechmeister.
Goals: Ringstead 2, Eglington, O'Farrell.

October 4, 1953   WCQ France (Paris)   Lost 3-5*   45,000

France: Vignal, Gianessi, Marche, Penverne, Jonquet, Marcel, Ujlaki, Glovacki, Kopa, Flamion, Piantoni.
Ireland: O'Neill, Dunne, Moroney, Martin, Aherne, Fitzsimons, Farrell, O'Farrell, Eglington, Walsh, Ryan.
Goals: Ryan, Walsh, O'Farrell (Republic of Ireland), Ujlaki 2, Glovacki, Penverne, Flamion (France).

May 1, 1955   Friendly v Holland (Dublin)   Won 1-0   16,680

Ireland: O'Neill, Martin, Donovan, Lawler, Fitzsimons, Eglington, O'Farrell, Ambrose, Gavin, Fitzgerald, Farrell.
Holland: Landman, Wiersma, Kuys, Steenbergen, Van der Hart, Klaessens, Wilkes, Schouten, Van der Gijp,
Timmermans, Geel. Goal: Fitzgerald.

May 25, 1955   Friendly v Norway (Oslo)   Won 3-1   18,574

Norway: Aronsen, Bakker, Berge, T.Olsen, Svenssen, Hernes, Hvidsten, Kristiansen, Kotte, Sorensen, W.Olsen.
Ireland: O'Neill, Fallon, Martin, Gannon, Donovan, Lawler, Fitzsimons, O'Farrell, Cummins, Ringstead, Glynn.
Goals: Cummins 2, Ringstead (Republic of Ireland), Kotte (Norway).

October 19, 1955   Friendly v Yugoslavia (Dublin)   Lost 1-4   22,000

Ireland: O'Neill, Martin, Lawler, Murphy, Fitzsimons, Tuohy, O'Farrell, Cummins, Ringstead, Farrell, Gibbons.
Yugoslavia: Beara, Belin, Zekovic, Boskov, Crnkovic, Krstic, Rajkov, Vukas, Milutinovic, Veselinovic, Zebec.
Goals: Fitzsimons (Republic of Ireland), Milutinovic 3, Veselinovic (Yugoslavia).

May 10, 1956   Friendly v Holland (Rotterdam)   Won 4-1   60,000

Holland: De Munck, Wiersma, Van der Hart, Odenthal, Brooymans, Klaessens, Appel, Bosselaar, Koopal, Lenstra,
Moulijn.
Ireland: O'Neill, Godwin, Dunne, Cantwell, Martin, Ringstead, Whelan, Fitzgerald, O'Farrell, Fitzsimons, Haverty.
Goals: Fitzsimons 2, Haverty, Ringstead (Republic of Ireland), Appel (Holland).

October 2, 1957   WCQ v Denmark (Copenhagen) Won 2-0   28,000

Denmark: From, Larsen, V.Nielsen, F.Nielsen, Andersen, Olsesen, Pedersen, Jensen, Hansen, Mosegaard, Kjaer.
Ireland: Dunne, Godwin, Hurley, Cantwell, Ringstead, Cummins, Saward, Fitzsimons, Haverty, O'Farrell, Curtis.
Goals: Cummins, Curtis.

May 10, 1959   ECQ v Czechoslovakia (Bratislava) Lost 0-4   60,000

Czechoslovakia: Stacho, Tichy, Popluhar, Novak, Matlak, Bubernik, Pavlovic, Scherer, Bubnik, Kaconi, Dolinsky.
Ireland: O'Neill, Cantwell, Whittaker, Hurley, McGrath, Ringstead, Hamilton, O'Farrell, Fitzsimons, Tuohy, Cummins.
Goals: Stacho (pen), Bubernik, Paulovic, Dolinsky.

__Frank (third in line) running out for his international debut against Austria in Vienna in 1952. Despite a 6-0 defeat, the Irish Independent said it was "one of the greatest displays of scientific soccer ever given by an Irish team."__

177

FRANK'S MANAGERIAL CAREER

Season	Club	Div (Pos.)
1961-62	Weymouth	SL (6th)
1962-63	Weymouth	SL (3rd)
1963-64	Weymouth	SL (7th)

Lost 5-2 on aggregate to Burton Albion in Southern League Cup final

1964-65	Weymouth	SL (1st)

Lost 3-1 on aggregate to Cambridge United in Southern League Cup final

1965-66	Torquay United	D4 (3rd)
1966-67	Torquay United	D3 (7th)
1967-68	Torquay United	D3 (4th)
1968-69	Torquay United - Left December 1968	D3 (6th)
1968-69	Leicester City - Joined December 1968	D1 (21st)

Lost 1-0 to Manchester City in FA Cup final at Wembley

1969-70	Leicester City	D2 (3rd)
1970-71	Leicester City	D2 (1st)
1971-72	Manchester United	D1 (8th)
1972-73	Manchester United - Left December 1972	D1 (18th)
1973-74	Cardiff City - Joined November 1973	D2 (17th)
1974-76	Iran *Won 1974 Asian Games, beating Israel 1-0 in final*	
1976-77	Torquay United - November 1976 to March 1977	D4 (16th)
1980	Al-Shaab (UAE)	N/A
1981-82	Torquay United as manager/general manager	D4 (15th)

FRANK'S UK MANAGERIAL RECORD

Club	Spell	G	W	D	L
Weymouth	1961-1965	210	106	43	61
Torquay United	1965-1968	175	79	39	57
Leicester City	1968-1971	134	62	42	30
Manchester United	1971-1972	81	30	24	27
Cardiff City	1973-1974	28	11	7	10
Torquay United	1976-1977	13	4	2	7
Torquay United	1981-1982	50	14	15	21

Weymouth results include Southern League, Southern League Cup and FA Cup. Torquay United, Leicester City, Manchester United and Cardiff City include Football League, League Cup, FA Cup and Welsh Cup. Friendlies and other cup competitions are not included.

SEASONS TO REMEMBER

PRESTON NORTH END, DIVISION ONE RUNNERS-UP 1957-58

	P	W	D	L	F	A	W	D	L	F	A	Pts
Wolverhampton W.	42	17	3	1	60	21	11	5	5	43	26	64
Preston North End	**42**	**18**	**2**	**1**	**63**	**14**	**8**	**5**	**8**	**37**	**37**	**59**
Tottenham Hotspur	42	13	4	4	58	33	8	5	8	35	44	51
West Bromwich Alb.	42	14	4	3	59	29	4	10	7	33	41	50
Manchester City	42	14	4	3	58	33	8	1	12	46	67	49
Burnley	42	16	2	3	52	21	5	3	13	28	53	47
Blackpool	42	11	2	8	47	35	8	4	9	33	32	44
Luton Town	42	13	3	5	45	22	6	3	12	24	41	44
Manchester United	42	10	4	7	45	31	6	7	8	40	44	43
Nottingham Forest	42	10	4	7	41	27	6	6	9	28	36	42
Chelsea	42	10	5	6	47	34	5	7	9	36	45	42
Arsenal	42	10	4	7	48	39	6	3	12	25	46	39
Birmingham City	42	8	6	7	43	37	6	5	10	33	52	39
Aston Villa	42	12	4	5	46	26	4	3	14	27	60	39
Bolton Wanderers	42	9	5	7	38	35	5	5	11	27	52	38
Everton	42	5	9	7	34	35	8	2	11	31	40	37
Leeds United	42	10	6	5	33	23	4	3	14	18	40	37
Leicester City	42	11	4	6	59	41	3	1	17	32	71	33
Newcastle United	42	6	4	11	38	42	6	4	11	35	39	32
Portsmouth	42	10	6	5	45	34	2	2	17	28	54	32
Sunderland	42	7	7	7	32	33	3	5	13	22	64	32
Sheffield Wednesday	42	12	2	7	45	40	0	5	16	24	52	31

WEYMOUTH, SOUTHERN LEAGUE CHAMPIONS 1964-65

	P	W	D	L	F	A	Pts
Weymouth	**42**	**24**	**8**	**10**	**99**	**50**	**56**
Guildford City	42	21	12	9	73	49	54
Worcester City	42	22	6	14	100	62	50
Yeovil Town	42	18	14	10	76	55	50
Chelmsford City	42	21	8	13	86	77	50
Margate	42	20	9	13	88	79	49
Dartford	42	17	11	14	74	64	45
Nuneaton Borough	42	19	7	16	57	55	45
Cambridge United	42	16	11	15	78	66	43
Bedford Town	42	17	9	16	66	70	43
Cambridge City	42	16	9	17	72	69	41
Cheltenham Town	42	15	11	16	72	78	41
Folkestone Town	42	17	7	18	72	79	41
Romford	42	17	7	18	61	70	41
King's Lynn	42	13	13	16	56	79	39
Tonbridge	42	10	16	16	66	75	36
Wellington Town	42	13	10	19	63	78	36
Rugby Town	42	15	6	21	71	98	36
Wisbech Town	42	14	6	22	75	91	34
Bexley United	42	14	5	23	67	74	33
Hastings United	42	9	14	19	58	86	32
Bath City	42	13	3	26	60	86	29

SEASONS TO REMEMBER

TORQUAY UNITED, PROMOTED FROM DIVISION FOUR, 1965-66

	P	W	D	L	F	A	W	D	L	F	A	Pts
Doncaster Rovers	46	15	6	2	49	21	9	5	9	36	33	59
Darlington	46	16	3	4	41	17	9	6	8	31	36	59
Torquay United	**46**	**17**	**2**	**4**	**43**	**20**	**7**	**8**	**8**	**29**	**29**	**58**
Colchester United	46	13	7	3	45	21	10	3	10	25	26	56
Tranmere Rovers	46	15	1	7	56	32	9	7	7	37	34	56
Luton Town	46	19	2	2	65	27	5	6	12	25	43	56
Chester City	46	15	5	3	52	27	5	7	11	27	43	52
Notts County	46	9	8	6	32	25	10	4	9	29	28	50
Newport County	46	14	6	3	46	24	4	6	13	29	51	48
Southport	46	15	6	2	47	20	3	6	14	21	49	48
Bradford PA	46	14	2	7	59	31	7	3	13	43	61	47
Barrow	46	12	8	3	48	31	4	7	12	24	45	47
Stockport County	46	12	4	7	42	29	6	2	15	29	41	42
Crewe Alexandra	46	12	4	7	42	23	4	5	14	19	40	41
Halifax Town	46	11	6	6	46	31	4	5	14	21	44	41
Barnsley	46	11	6	6	43	24	4	4	15	31	54	40
Aldershot	46	12	6	5	47	27	3	4	16	28	57	40
Hartlepools United	46	13	4	6	44	22	3	4	16	19	53	40
Port Vale	46	12	7	4	38	18	3	2	18	10	41	39
Chesterfield	46	8	9	6	37	35	5	4	14	25	43	39
Rochdale	46	12	1	10	46	27	4	4	15	25	60	37
Lincoln City	46	9	7	7	37	29	4	4	15	20	53	37
Bradford City	46	10	5	8	37	34	2	8	13	26	60	37
Wrexham	46	10	4	9	43	43	3	5	15	29	61	35

LEICESTER CITY, DIVISION TWO CHAMPIONS 1970-71

	P	W	D	L	F	A	W	D	L	F	A	Pts
Leicester City	**42**	**12**	**7**	**2**	**30**	**14**	**11**	**6**	**4**	**27**	**16**	**59**
Sheffield United	42	14	6	1	49	18	7	8	6	24	21	56
Cardiff City	42	12	7	2	39	16	8	6	7	25	25	53
Carlisle United	42	16	3	2	39	13	4	10	7	26	30	53
Hull City	42	11	5	5	31	16	8	8	5	23	25	51
Luton Town	42	12	7	2	40	18	6	6	9	22	25	49
Middlesbrough	42	13	6	2	37	16	4	8	9	23	27	48
Millwall	42	13	5	3	36	12	6	4	11	23	30	47
Birmingham City	42	12	7	2	30	12	5	5	11	28	36	46
Norwich City	42	11	8	2	34	20	4	6	11	20	32	44
QPR	42	11	5	5	39	22	5	6	10	31	16	43
Swindon Town	42	12	7	2	38	14	3	5	13	23	37	42
Sunderland	42	11	6	4	34	21	4	6	11	18	33	42
Oxford United	42	8	8	5	23	23	6	6	9	18	25	42
Sheffield Wednesday	42	10	7	4	32	27	2	5	14	19	42	36
Portsmouth	42	9	4	8	32	28	1	10	10	14	33	34
Orient	42	5	11	5	16	15	4	5	12	13	36	34
Watford	42	6	7	8	18	22	4	6	11	20	38	33
Bristol City	42	9	6	6	30	28	1	5	15	16	36	31
Charlton Athletic	42	7	6	8	28	30	1	8	12	13	35	30
Blackburn Rovers	42	5	8	8	20	28	1	7	13	17	41	27
Bolton Wanderers	42	6	5	10	22	31	1	5	15	13	43	24

"Football can be like the seasons. You have your springs, your summers and your winters. The secret is to hold on and know that if you have been honest, the weather will change."

FRANK O'FARRELL